SO-ADT-925

Alastair Sawday's

GUIDE TO
SPECIAL
PARIS HOTELS

ASP
Alastair Sawday Publishing

ACKNOWLEDGEMENTS

Rarely can an acknowledgement have been easier. One person has researched, written and produced this guide. I have offered occasional encouragement and support as publisher, but there it ends. This is Ann Cooke-Yarborough's book. Can you imagine the rigours not only of dealing diplomatically with legions of Paris hoteliers but also of inspecting scores and scores of hotels, some of which were banal, monotone and hostile? Imagine, too, the hectares of corporate carpet, the anonymous cubicles, the batallions of tired receptionists. It is not easy. Throughout it all, Ann retained her sense of humour and her judgement where I, for one, would have lost both in a fog of confused memories.

She has an unerring eye for detail and a rare ability to see things in their historical and cultural context. As well as a deep understanding of the "aesthetic", she draws on a rich Anglo-French culture when she writes. Her 30 years in France have equipped her to reach instinctively for the peculiar Frenchness of a hotel, and for its humanity; you can feel both qualities in this book.

Others have contributed, of course. The cartoons by **John Pruen** are a particular delight, line drawings taken from his French vocabulary notebooks. This selection – affectionate, witty and sensitive – is the first to be published.

Managing Editor:	Ann Cooke-Yarborough
Researcher:	Ann Cooke-Yarborough
Assistant researcher:	Lucy Nérot
Data processing/admin.:	Ann Cooke-Yarborough
Typesetting/Reprographics:	Avonset, Midsomer Norton, nr Bath
Printing:	BPC, Paulton, Avon
Distribution:	Portfolio
Design and maps:	Springboard Design, Bristol
Colour illustrations and symbols:	Celia Witchard
Cartoons:	John Pruen
Back-up photographs:	Eliophot, Aix-en-Pce (No13);
	Ann Cooke-Yarborough
Accounts/admin.:	Sheila Clifton
Inspiration:	Jane Ryder and Richard Binns

DISCLAIMER

We make no claims to pure objectivity in judging hotels. Our opinions and tastes are ours alone and this book is a statement of them; yet we hope that you will share them.

We have done our utmost to get our facts right but apologise unreservedly for any mistakes that may have crept in. Sometimes, too, prices shift, usually upwards, and "things" change. We would be grateful to be told of any errors and changes, however small.

INTRODUCTION

Paris hoteliers are a special breed. Those who blend warmth, professionalism and individuality are an endangered species. This book celebrates them.

There are dozens of books about Paris; they tell you what to see, do, eat, visit, buy and love. Strangely, they largely avoid telling you where to stay. That could just be because it is hard to make choices. If you have read my Guide to French Bed & Breakfast, you will know what sort of places I like. Many people, it seems, share my willingness to take small risks. So I have taken the plunge and tried the same approach in Paris, a mine-field for the unwary.

A problem with Paris is that, however wonderful your day, it can be too easily spoiled by an expensively rotten night. And if, like me, you have an aversion to bad taste and bad manners an otherwise comfortable hotel can make no excuses. An exquisite hotel is made less so by an ice-maiden or a surly youth at the reception desk.

So this book sets out to introduce you to some of the nicest, least pretentious, best-value hotels in the City of Light. We hope we have left out the very grand, the pompous, the poor value, the clinically modern, the unfriendly, the ordinary.

We have searched for the hotels that we think represent the best of the Paris hotel scene. The city has a long history of looking after visitors; it also has a long history of cynicism, off-ripping, overbearing behaviour and downright rudeness. Yet it has been fun to discover how many small hotels have bravely hung on to a way of receiving people that I feared might have gone the way of...the footpaths beside the Seine.

The sheer humanity of many hotel-keepers has been an inspiration. Their ability to maintain values in the 1990s hotel jungle is impressive and deserves the support of you, gentle reader, when you next go to Paris. Don't, please, go to a chain hotel; they destroy so much that you probably value. Don't spend your money on the big names, even if their radical price-cutting tactics seem seductive. Their first casualty is that very humanity.

Treat yourself – and go to those who are happy to welcome you, attend to you, help you have a wonderful holiday and not charge the earth for it.

Inclusion
What I have said above gives the main clue to how we choose hotels: we have to LIKE them. Some have declined to pay the small fee we charge to feature in this book, often because it is a first edition, but the majority that we have liked have been happy to join us in making the guide possible.

HOW TO USE THIS BOOK –
GENERAL FACTS OF PARIS HOTEL LIFE

John Pruen's Cartoons
Just enjoy them – and don't look for any particular relevance. They are, by the way, entirely original and have never been seen in print before.

Telephones
With few exceptions, all rooms have telephones, some with direct dialling. Remember to use hotel telephones only in extremis or if you are rich. The bills rarely fail to raise eyebrows and temperatures.

<u>Telephone numbers</u> given are valid until 17 October 1996. Then, France will adopt the international code of 00 for dialling other countries. All French numbers will have 10 digits; for calls within France, the country will be divided into 5 regions, each with a code. The code for Paris will be 01 so from inside France, a Paris number will be 01 followed by the old 8-digit number; from outside France, the same preceded by 00 (this is the information we have at the time of going to press).

Family suites
Many hotels can turn two double rooms into a self-contained "apartment" so do enquire when booking.

Bathrooms
Almost all bathrooms have wcs so we have only specified the exceptions. Where some rooms have just bath or just shower, we have said so. Be prepared for the smallest cubicle in some of the cheaper hotels and even in some of the others...

Noise
Noise is a fairly general problem in Paris. A pair of cooing lovers below your window (or, more annoyingly, a stream of hooting cars) is often part of the Paris package. More and more hotels are fitting double glazing or double windows but if you are a fresh air fiend and can't sleep with closed windows, bring your earplugs. Alternatively, specify that you want a room "sur la cour" or away from the noise ("loin du bruit"). Some absolutely delightful places don't have such a thing so you have to make your choice.

Space
The greatest luxury in Paris is **SPACE.** Each square metre is worth its weight in good gold francs. You will understand its value when you try a selection of our 3-stars and see the enormous variety in space per person per room.

Breakfast
There is continental and there is buffet. Buffet means anything from continental + eggs to a vast spread worth breakfast, lunch and half of dinner in one go. Where a buffet is offered it is taken in the breakfast room. If you choose to have breakfast in your room it will probably be continental and cost the same price. Some hotels never used to have space for a breakfast room – you had it in your bedroom. Works, improvements and fashion have encouraged many to throw open their underparts and create the ubiquitous Parisian 3-star vaulted-cellar breakfast room. They are always "fascinating", "authentic", original-foundation-level "experiences" with fine masonry and interesting olde worlde decorative effects to match. But they can be very stuffy and close and not necessarily the place to start the day, far from the light and air of the morning. You can always have breakfast in your room; you are the sole judge.

Service
The second greatest luxury is **SERVICE**, that properly attentive approach that is never servile nor obsequious but neither is it so relaxed as to become casual or even offhand. Parisians are intense, intelligent, ambitious – and pretty attentive to themselves and their own needs and aims. When you meet a really friendly hotel-keeper or receptionist, do please tell them how much you appreciate their attitude. It is exceptional. We have tried to keep this as a criterion of selection although the same people do not work at the desk every day and the same individual is not so sunny every morning. We have eliminated

some potentially good hotels because the telephone reception was surly to the point of rudeness, or the management was singularly absent leaving a miserable minion to hold the fort, or our meeting was too cold and distant for us to want to pursue the relationship.

The luxy "palaces" where high couturiers and film stars go to be seen and photographed may pay small fortunes for uniform designs but forget to teach the wearers the basics of common civility, the first lesson of which is that each human being deserves the warmth of genuine recognition. Snooty, condescending or ice-cold treatment is NOT service, however much you pay for it.

Expectations of service
We have selected hotels for their friendliness above all, so service should be an aspect of the welcome. But the smaller hotels have small staffs so don't be surprised if a gin and tonic isn't available at 2 am.

Pillows and tea
Those long things (which you once used to separate yourself from your kid sister on family holidays?) still exist but there is usually a nicer pillow hidden in the cupboard. If not, ASK for it; don't suffer in silence. If only coffee is on offer at breakfast and you drink only tea, don't start 3 days in misery and frustration; ASK for tea : there will always be a tea-bag forthcoming.

Tipping
Don't be bullied! Only tip if someone has made a special effort for you.

TECHNICAL BITS AND PIECES

The star system
It is somewhat misleading. The majority of small hotels in Paris have 3 official stars. Stars are allocated by totally bureaucratic minima of square metres of bathroom per bedroom, width of walking space around beds, number of taps per person, and so on. So a category might cover the sublime to the ridiculous. Similarly, 4 stars SHOULD mean better than 3. Some of our 3s, however, are more luxurious – in space, quality of welcome, attention to detail and services available – than the lesser 4-stars which have gained their medals by the skin of their teeth, half centimetre measurements and bits of equipment.

Prices
In general, we give the advertised standard rates. Most hotels offer reductions for low-season stays (August, July, winter, except professional show periods,...), long stays, etc. Some (the most successful? the most honest? the proudest?) will not offer a single special price, but they are few and far between. So always ask.

Also, this Guide may cover two seasons. The prices given are correct to our knowledge at the time of going to press and valid for 1996 but hotel owners and managers have every right to alter their rates at any time. Some hotels may change their prices for 1997 or even during 1996, taxation levels may change for them all, breakfast may become more copious and vastly more expensive. Always check when you book as we cannot guarantee the prices quoted.

Coding
S = single; D = double; T = twin; TR = triple; Q = quadruple; DP = duplex; ST = suite or apartment.

Taxe de séjour

A tax per person per night in Paris hotels was imposed by the City Council in 1994. At present it stands at 3F for 1-star, 5F for 2-star, 6F for 3-star and 7F for 4-star. Some of the prices in our guide include this tax, some don't – the rule is unclear and we cannot specifiy which solution each hotel has adopted. So be prepared for the possibility of a small extra sum per day on your bill.

Booking services (Services de Concierge)

All 4-star, most 3-star and some lesser-starred hotels will deal with reservations for theatres, restaurants, trains, etc but only the 4-stars are bound to do so .

Currency exchange

The smarter hotels have an exchange rate board at reception; others will give you francs for your own currency as a personal service; some won't touch it. In all cases, you will get a worse rate than at the bank as the hotel has to cover itself for fluctuations between time of transaction and time of deposit.

Trends

There is a trend towards standardised "comfort" that is bound to remove some of the individuality from those little old Paris hotels. This is due in great part to competition from the multinational chains with their factory-style plastic-smile establishments. The small independent places now believe that they can only attract American clients in summer – when they most need them – if they have air conditioning (this can mean rebuilding ceilings, removing old panelling, changing bathrooms), more little bits of toiletries, etc. It also means going to the hotel industry's annual show to choose deeper pile carpets, more "fashionable" curtain material, more "acceptable" light fittings with dimmer switches, and other elements of standardisation.

The heavy outlay brings more debt and worry and lowers the owner/manager's enjoyment of his job. This it turn tends to make him less open to his guests, liable to consider them as little more than providers of cash to pay off the loan. The supermarket v high-street-shop battle is being played out again here and the next generation may only know chain-operated hotels, the family businesses having died of discouragement.

Long live the family-run 1-star hotel with no telephone or television in your bedroom, a simple shower cabin, loo down the corridor (they aren't ***all*** ghastly) and vast riches of history and conversation and friendship.

There is another trend, however, which we welcome. It is the growth of small hotels that, while modern, are exciting experiments in design, colour and form. Paris has more of these than most European cities and some of them add excitement to this book.

HINTS & TIPS

These may hold for all of France or be specifically relevant to Paris. We hope they will make your stay less fraught and more memorable for lack of silly practical hitches or real ripoffs.

Travelling in Paris

Our maps are not intended to help you get around Paris. Bring or buy one of the Indispensable ™, Taride™, Michelin or other pocket street atlases and get the excellent map of the metro and bus routes free from a metro station.

Don't use your car. It will cost you a fortune in parking fees (or fines), years off your life in frustration and fury before finding a parking spot. Sitting in traffic jams, adding your bit to the already dangerous levels of pollution in the city, is no way to spend ANY of your holiday.

Do use the excellent public transport system. It is well worth taking the trouble to understand how the buses work. Some bus routes take you past the great monuments. Also, in contrast to the guided tours, you can *get off and on when you like!* They go faster, too, thanks to a lengthy system of bus lanes.

The metro is fast, efficient, clean, safe and cheap. The stations are close together and trains are frequent. Paris has the virtue, for visitors, of being a very dense city. There are several forms of short, medium and long-stay passes. Your hotel will tell you where to find out.

Taxis are, for the impecunious, a last resort. However, they are allowed to use the bus lanes...

Pharmaceuticals, cosmetics, etc.

Do be aware that a French "Pharmacie" sells only certain brands of cosmetics and toiletries at high prices. So use the supermarkets' cosmetics and para-pharmaceuticals shelves to replace the toothbrush you forgot, buy a bottle of vitamins or try out a French lipstick.

Posting letters

Post boxes are yellow, post offices are recognisable by a luminous yellow sign with a stylized bluebird flashed across it. They usually stay open till 6 or 7 pm.

Refreshments

Paris cafés tend to be expensive. But do remember that black coffee is the cheapest drink of all and a glass of plonk usually the second cheapest; all soft drinks cost more (you pay for the name) and tea , traditionally the beverage of wealthy fashionable ladies, is scandalously overpriced. Don't use up too much energy railing against it. Prices double, by the way, when you sit at a table; few cafés have bar stools but if you can bear to stand at the "zinc" counter for your "demi" (of beer), you will be able to have twice as many for your daily drinks money.

Information in English

The Paris Tourist Office produces a book in English called *Paris Users' Guide* to help visitors find or do anything they want to do or find in the city. You can also get information, in English or French, by telephone. The number is (33) 1 44 29 12 12; the line is open Monday-Friday, 8am-8pm.

YOUR COMMENTS

We include a report form at the back of the book. We are eager for all kinds of feedback. Please write and tell us your experiences, good or bad, in "our" hotels and your reactions to our Guide. Give it to us "straight"! We would also be delighted to hear of your own recommendations. (If you are worried about revealing a little-known favourite, remember that this book may encourage the creation of other hotels like it.)

Useful Vocabulary

**Some useful words and expressions
to help you avoid ending up like this** ·····················▶

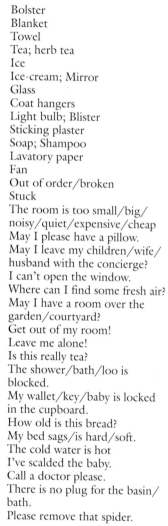

**Paumé
Dropout; lost case**

Bolster	*Un Traversin*
Blanket	*Une Couverture*
Towel	*Une Serviette*
Tea; herb tea	*Un Thé; Une Infusion*
Ice	*De la glace*
Ice-cream; Mirror	*Une glace*
Glass	*Un Verre*
Coat hangers	*Des Cintres*
Light bulb; Blister	*Une Ampoule*
Sticking plaster	*Du Sparadrap (sic)*
Soap; Shampoo	*Du Savon; Du Shampooing*
Lavatory paper	*Du Papier toilette*
Fan	*Un Ventilateur*
Out of order/broken	*En panne/cassé*
Stuck	*Coincé*
The room is too small/big/ noisy/quiet/expensive/cheap	*La chambre est trop petite/grande/ bruyante/tranquille/chère/bon marché.*
May I please have a pillow.	*Je voudrais un oreiller, s'il vous plaît.*
May I leave my children/wife/ husband with the concierge?	*Pourrais-je laisser mes enfants/ma femme/ mon mari avec le concierge?*
I can't open the window.	*Je n'arrive pas à ouvrir la fenêtre.*
Where can I find some fresh air?	*Où peut-on trouver un peu d'air?*
May I have a room over the garden/courtyard?	*Je voudrais une chambre sur le jardin/la cour.*
Get out of my room!	*Sortez de ma chambre!*
Leave me alone!	*Laissez-moi tranquille!*
Is this really tea?	*C'est vraiment du thé ça?*
The shower/bath/loo is blocked.	*La douche/la baignoire/le wc est bouché.*
My wallet/key/baby is locked in the cupboard.	*J'ai enfermé mon porte-monnaie/ma clé/mon bébé dans l'armoire.*
How old is this bread?	*De quand date ce pain?*
My bed sags/is hard/soft.	*Mon lit est défoncé/trop dur/trop mou.*
The cold water is hot	*L'eau froide est chaude.*
I've scalded the baby.	*J'ai échaudé le bébé.*
Call a doctor please.	*Appelez un médecin s'il vous plaît.*
There is no plug for the basin/ bath.	*Il n'y a pas de bouchon pour le lavabo/ la baignoire.*
Please remove that spider.	*Enlevez cette araignée, s'il vous plaît.*

Je vais faire la grasse matinée.	I'm going to have a lie in.
J'en ai ras le bol.	I'm fed up (with this).
J'en ai marre.	I'm sick of this.
C'est marrant ça.	That's funny (peculiar or ha!ha!).
Se marrer.	To laugh.
Oh la vache!	What a cow!/Oh lord!/How awful!
C'est vachement bien ça.	That's really great.

Explanation of the symbols

Treat each one as a guide rather than a concrete indicator. A few notes:

 A green leafy spot It might be a tiny bright-white plant-filled lightwell; very occasionally it is a fully-fledged garden.

 English spoken by receptionist and management, but not necessarily by the other staff.

 Pets are accepted as long as they are properly trained and docile. There may be a supplement to pay.

 Credit cards Most major credit cards accepted. Any exceptions are specified.

 Lift installed. It may stop short of the top floor or start on the first floor.

 Bar There is a bar or simply bar service.

 Mini bar in bedrooms.

 Restaurant The hotel has its own restaurant or a separately-managed restaurant on the spot or next door.

 Room service for light meals (or more) delivered to your room by outside caterers or the hotel kitchen.

 Double glazing Rooms (on street side at least) have double glazing or double windows.

 Air conditioning in bedrooms. It may be by a fully-integrated centrally-operated system or individual apparatus.

 Television set in bedrooms.

 Hair dryer in bedrooms.

 Safe in bedrooms (otherwise you can leave your valuables at reception).

CONTENTS

Paris – General Map

Detailed maps are shown on the following pages.

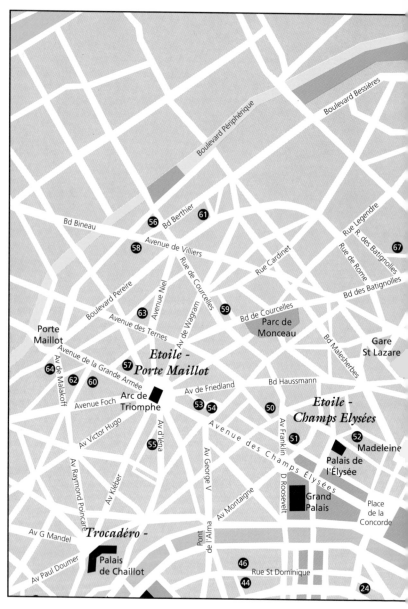

MAP 1

Scale

1 km

1 mile

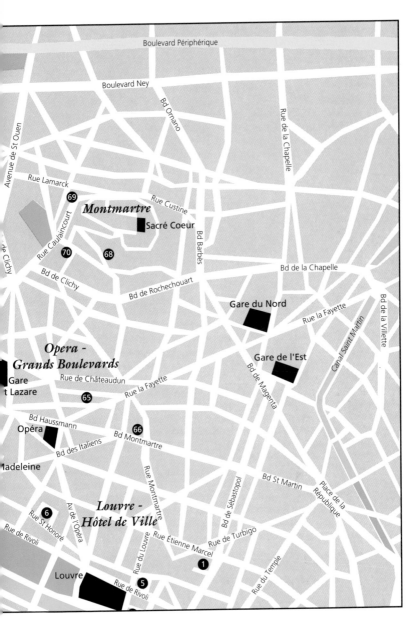

MAP 2

MAP 3

Scale

1 mile

1 km

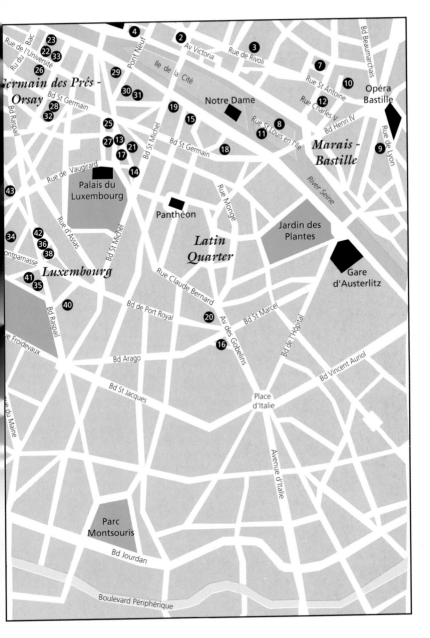

MAP 4

Other *Alastair Sawday's Guides*

Alastair Sawday's
GUIDE TO

French Bed & Breakfast

2ND EDITION
... *bigger and even better*

Over 500 homes, the elegant and the simple, from châteaux to farm houses ... all of value and character.

Beyond Paris lies the rest of France; this guide leads you through 'deepest' France to encounters with the French in all the Frenchness and warmth of their beautiful homes.

Friendly descriptions of over 500 hosts and homes; details of rooms, prices and meals; the whole of France in 16 regions, with clear maps, directions and reference systems.

Each B&B is illustrated with a colour photograph. The guide is available in all major bookshops. Price: £11.95

Alastair Sawday's Guide to Special Places to Stay in Spain

The Spanish hotel 'scene' bristles with hazards for the unwary. Choose from among the most attractive and interesting hotels throughout Spain, each illustrated with two colour photographs. (Publication May 1996).

Rue de Rivoli & Tuileries Gardens
•
Palais Royal
•
Forum des Halles
•
St Eustache
•
Pompidou Centre
•
St Germain l'Auxerrois

Louvre – Hôtel de Ville

Parachever

Put the finishing touches to

Etre dans l'embarras

Be embarrassed

 exc Diners

Hôtel Agora

* *

7 rue de la Cossonnerie
Paris
75001

Tel: (1)42 33 46 02
Fax: (1)42 33 80 99

Management: Monsieur Fresnel, Monsieur de Marco.

Look well, oh traveller — the door is hard to find between hot dog shop and bank, under the feathery acacias of the pedestrian area. You are greeted on entering by a delicious cherub showing the way up an elegant grey staircase to the reception. Old and modern are thus married throughout. Alongside a sober contemporary desk there is an elaborate gilt mirror, a carved armchair, a golden cage and plants galore. The welcome combines old-fashioned grace and modern friendliness in this gentle salon overlooking the lively street — we loved the feel. The tiny breakfast room is to scale, its huge floral pattern less so. All the rooms are different, some smaller than others but none very big; all give onto the street, all have double glazing but if you sleep open-windowed, ask for a high floor. Beds have new firm foam mattresses and curtains are all white. There are choice 19th-century engravings everywhere, such as a very full-fleshed Judgement of Paris offset by a demure Virgin Mary. Colour contrasts abound too: yellow red-flowered wallpaper with blue frieze plus blue carpet and bedcover in No 51 which also has a lobby with cupboards, a balcony and a superb view of St Eustache. There are fine, carved, gilded, wall-mounted bedheads; one room has puce paintwork, soft mauvy walls and a leopard-skin chair. It all works admirably. The touch is very sure. Bathrooms are colourful and adequate. Altogether excellent value so close to the Pompidou Centre.

Rooms: 29 with shower or bath.
Price: S 360-565F; D 490-595F.
Breakfast: 35F.
Meals: None.
Metro: Les Halles; RER Châtelet-Les Halles.
Bus routes: 38 47
Car park: Les Halles.

The cage once held live birds, banned since American animal rightists stayed here during their campaign against the French fur trade and used gentle persuasion...

(1)

Map No: 2

Hôtel Britannique ★ ★ ★

20 avenue Victoria
Paris
75001

Tel: (1)42 33 74 59
Fax: (1)42 33 82 65

Management: J-F Danjou.

In the very middle of Paris, on the one quiet street beside the Châtelet, several generations of British Baxters owned this well-placed comfortable hotel and ran it exclusively for British clients... The present owner is an ex-naval man, with a passion for Turner whose "Jessica" greets you from her window in the lobby, whose sea scenes adorn the bedroom walls and whose "Fighting Temeraire" dominates the saloon-like sitting-room (alongside a model galleon, a "Crystal Palace" birdcage housing a lone dove and an EMI gramophone horn). There is a lush feel about the hallways but do use the staircase, elegantly pink and grey with lovely original fitted oak chests on each landing. The rooms are gently decorated with built-in elements, pastel walls, Laura Ashley materials, boxes of pot-pourri for extra florality and perfectly adequate bathrooms. Duvets are soon to replace blankets and bedcovers. The higher floors offer views over the surrounding roofs and the treetops of the avenue below where garden plants, furniture and birds are still sold. But it is the reception areas that make this place — and the warm reception guests receive. The semi-basement breakfast room is lit by a well of greenery and in a glass case you can admire a silver teapot presented to the Baxters "at Whitsuntide 1861 by their Scarborough friends".

Rooms: 40 with bath or shower.
Price: S 626-752F; D 752-862F;
TR 958F.
Breakfast: 50F for a copious buffet.
Meals: None.
Metro: Châtelet; RER Châtelet-Les Halles.
Bus routes: 21 38 47 58 75 76 81
Car park: Hôtel de Ville.

During the First World War this hotel was offered to American and English Quaker volunteers tending civilian victims — a Quaker service in wars the world over.

Map No: 4

  Visa only

Hôtel de Nice   **
42bis rue de Rivoli
Paris
75004

Tel: (1)42 78 55 29
Fax: (1)42 78 36 07

Management: Monsieur & Madame Voudoux.

You cannot but warm to the Voudoux and their lovely hotel. They both left high-flying professions to indulge their collectionitis and dream of running a "guest-house" together. It will feel like home from home for some: no television in bedrooms, Indian cotton covers on beds...and tent-like on the drawing-room ceiling, Numdah rugs on floors, a vast portrait of Lady Diana Cooper on one wall (bought, unknown and unmounted, for her beauty and style), innumerable prints, engravings and mirrors on others and a remarkable sense of hospitality — the art of intelligent conversation is still alive. The discreet door is blue, the hallway and stairs decorated with deep red bookbinding paper, turquoise paintwork and 19th-century views of capital cities, some wildly imaginary (Peking-on-sea). Rooms have pretty Laura Ashley papers copied from French 18th-century designs and mix 'n match curtains, old doors on built-in cupboards — Monsieur has a passion for old doors, polished or painted — portraits of ancestors and old bedside lights. None of the rooms is very large; storage space is adequate for sensible travellers; bathrooms, also quite small, are modern and properly equipped. If the hosts and the public areas are fairly exotic, the bedrooms are fresh, individual and restful except for their windows...which all overlook the little square just off the rue de Rivoli and let in the noise when open. But the Nice is excellent value.

Rooms: 23 with bath or shower.
Price: S 350F; D (small) 380F;
D (larger) or T 400F.
Breakfast: 30 F.
Meals: None.
Metro: Hôtel de Ville; RER Châtelet-Les Halles.
Bus routes: 47 69 72 74 76 96
Car park: Lobeau & Baudoyer.

In rue du Bourg Tibourg is the beautiful 1830s shop where Mariage Frères sell innumerable teas in black tins and serve wickedly tempting cakes in the tea room.

③   **Map No:** 4

Le Relais du Louvre ★ ★ ★

19 rue des Prêtres St Germain l'Auxerrois
Paris
75001

Tel: (1)40 41 96 42
Fax: (1)40 41 96 44

Management: Sophie Aulnette.

An utterly delightful place, with a charming young manageress and views down the throats of Gothic gargoyles! Loaded with history — the French Revolutionaries printed their newspaper in the cellar; it was Puccini's Café Momus in "Bohême" — the building daily rings with the famous carillon from the belfry beside St Germain l'Auxerrois. Beams abound. The lobby is large, airy and colourful in red and green. The low reception desk provides for a warm direct welcome. Old pieces of furniture and oriental rugs add to the modern advantages of excellent bedding and fully-equipped bathrooms (a few singles have showers only). Streetside rooms look out over the pure Flamboyant-style ogive windows, pinnacles and flying buttresses (or 'flying buttocks' as I heard a child innocently call them) of the church; look left and you see the austerely grandiose neo-Classical façade of the Louvre. Other rooms give onto a plant and light-filled patio and two ground-floor rooms have direct access. Televisions hide in padded stools. The top-floor junior suites have twin beds and a sofa, pastel walls, exuberant-print upholstery, good storage space and lots of light from their mansard windows. You feel secluded and coddled. Other rooms are smaller but still luminous, fresh and restful. On each floor two rooms can become a family suite. The sense of service is highly developed and as there is no breakfast room breakfast comes to you.

Rooms: 20, inc 2 suites, with bath or shower.
Price: S 600-750F; D 800-900F; ST 1280-1450F.
Breakfast: 50F.
Meals: Light meals 30-100F.
Metro: Louvre-Rivoli, Pont Neuf; RER Chatelet-Les Halles.
Bus routes: 68 69 72
Car park: Card at hotel.

The best view over Paris is just beside you — and it's free! Take the lift to the terrace roof of the Samaritaine store and admire the city from its very centre.

Tonic Hôtel Louvre   * *

12-14 rue du Roule
Paris
75001

Tel: (1)42 33 00 71
Fax: (1)40 26 06 86

Management: Frédéric Boissier.

People keep coming back to the Tonic for two things: its position, plumb in the heart (or belly when the great market was still here) of Paris, and its steam-and-jacuzzi baths, exceptional in a 2-star hotel. When you get back from conscientiously tramping round the Louvre or, if your children make you, round Disneyland, remove the stress of the day with a water massage + steam cure. We found the lobby rather bare but the energetic and friendly receptionists are ready to help you with any practical questions. The armchaired, ground-floor daylit breakfast room/bar looks onto life in the street (Frédéric Boissier sticks to his principles and refuses basement breakfast because it does nothing to stimulate you for the day). The hotel is in two adjacent buildings that communicate along the pavement. The older, more "traditional" half has more style and slightly higher prices. The hall here is old and gracious, the staircase, crafted in an unusual long curved V, is listed. Your legs will recognize the authentically worn oak nosings and terracotta tiles (take care or the lift!). Rooms are sparse and functional (decent storage in all), with high beamed ceilings, bare stone walls, copies of period furniture and no pictures. Rooms on "the other side" have the same fully-equipped and "tonic" bathrooms plus the basics of beds, table, chairs, room to move around and, on the top floor, a sense of light, a sloping ceiling and a balcony onto St Eustache, floodlit at night.

Rooms: 34 with jacuzzi and steam bath (except 2).
Price: S 450-850F; D 490-890F; TR 550-950F.
Breakfast: 30F included.
Meals: None.
Metro: Pont-Neuf, Louvre-Rivoli. RER Châtelet-Les Halles.
Bus routes: 21 67 69 72 74 75 76 81 96
Car park: St Eustache; Les Halles.

In rue de l'Arbre Sec, the "Dry Tree Inn", named after an evergreen tree in Palestine that lost its leaves the day Christ was crucified, used to receive Holy Land pilgrims.

5   **Map No: 2**

Hôtel des Tuileries   ★ ★ ★
10 rue Saint-Hyacinthe
Paris
75001

Tel: (1)42 61 04 17
Fax: (1)49 27 91 56

Management: Jean-Jacques Vidal.

There are antique oriental rugs everywhere — but mostly on walls; may they last for ever, they are so appropriate in this lovely quiet old building whose façade moves skywards in a rhythmic play of balconies, arches, cornices and mouldings. The huge doors give onto a white hall with rugs, mirrors, pictures old and new and, rather to our dismay, a modern reception desk and rather cool welcome. But we were comforted by the elegant, small-scale sitting areas and lovingly-kept plants in the lightwell that lights both ground floor and basement breakfast room (with its wall-hanging). The curving generous staircase is listed too and properly fitted with central runner and brass rods on polished wood. This place has been loved by the Vidal family for three generations now. In the bedrooms, the orientalising/chinoiserie element is fairly general but never to excess. It is found in Chinese vase table lamps, in Chinese-inspired wallpaper and paisley-pattern draperies. Care has been taken over colour matches — one white room has dark blue carpet, pale blue damask curtains and bedcover with a richly coloured rug on the wall behind the cane bedhead. The bedside lighting is good, there are pieces of old furniture plus some modern elements. One room has an interesting long narrow dressing table in carved painted wood and Empire bed and armchairs. Finally, the interior sprung mattresses are excellent and the marble bathrooms quite acceptable.

Rooms: 26 with bathrooms.
Price: S 590-790F; D 790-1200F; ST 1200-1800F.
Breakfast: 60F.
Meals: None.
Metro: Tuileries, Pyramides; RER Opéra-Auber.
Bus routes: 72
Car park: Place Vendôme.

The house was built for one of Marie-Antoinette's ladies-in-waiting; the supremely elegant, feminine façade and great carved front doors are listed and admirable indeed.

Marais – Bastille

Camper
Camp

Camper
Portray (with quick sure strokes)

exc AE Diners

Grand Hôtel Jeanne d'Arc ★ ★

3 rue de Jarente
Paris
75004

Tel: (1)48 87 62 11
Fax: (1)48 87 37 31

Management: Madame Mésenge.

From the outside, you might think you were in a small country town. The street is quiet, the buildings modest (with Parisian modesty), the window boxes flowing with greenery. And inside, the impression deepens. The first room you see is the breakfast room. On a corner with generous windows that are equally generously draped with billowing white muslin, it is furnished with café tables and chairs for a simple breakfast; the crocheted table cloths are the only reminder of the days when the hotel was known for its baroque profusion of doilies and antimacassars. Opposite is the reception where you will be quietly greeted by the friendly owner and staff. Then the surprise, the unexpected contrast : their very own escutcheon, a dazzling concoction of mirror, mosaic, glass danglers and electric candles. The combination of understated ordinariness and ventures into other realms of taste is the hallmark of the Jeanne d'Arc. The little lounge at the end of the corridor was hand-painted by an artist friend, the door numbers by another. The rest of the decor is unremarkable, perfectly fitting for a good-value two-star hotel. The colour schemes are very mixed (one room sports blue, orange, red, yellow and green all together), the room sizes vary considerably, but beds are good quality, quiet is guaranteed, you are a step away from the delightful tree-shaded Place du Marché Sainte Catherine and two from the Place des Vosges.

Rooms: 36 with bath or shower.
Price: S 300-385F; D 390-460F;
TR 515F.
Breakfast: 35F.
Meals: None.
Metro: St-Paul, Bastille; RER
Châtelet-Les Halles.
Bus routes: 29 96 69 76.
Car park: 19 rue St-Antoine.

The medieval "francs-bourgeois" were not open-minded middle-class gents but destitute citizens, exempted from taxation and housed in a nearby institution.

(7) **Map No:** 4

Hôtel du Jeu de Paume ★★★★
54 rue Saint-Louis-en-l'Ile
Paris
75004

Tel: (1)43 26 14 18
Fax: (1)40 46 02 76

Management: Elyane Prache.

There is only one like this — a lobby three storeys high and open to the timbers, the original indoor tennis court. And full of the owners' ideas, dreams and finds. 4 stars, small rooms, basic linen and oodles of atmosphere. You love it or you definitely don't. Love it for the shapes, eccentricities, aesthetic ironies, perfect secluded peace and sense of home, or feel unhappy with its unconventional attitudes, very relaxed staff (plus sheepdog Enzo) and often limited storage space. Seclusion? You easily miss the two brass plates into the porch. Peace? The hotel is built round a courtyard garden — all the rooms give onto courtyards. The original 17th-century timbers lift the eyes to unexpected heights (three lovely levels at the peak) over the old Provençal breakfast tables, creating an outdoor space indoors, with four former cloister columns, a courtyard wall-fountain and a stone cherub to remind you. A clear-sided lift and open spiral stairs reinforce the transparency. The main sitting/bar area is a family drawing room: deep leather sofas round a carved fireplace, bits of art and artefacts. Rooms are all different, mostly smallish with careful pastel and print decor, adequate bathrooms and well-sprung beds. Beams, real old floor tiles and visible stonework are all over. Duplexes have tiny staircases but more storage than others. Corner rooms on the top floor show the building's beautiful timber skeleton. It is a delight.

Rooms: 32, inc suites & duplexes, with bathrooms.
Price: S/D small 820-895F, standard 1195F, large 1295F; TR 1395F.
Breakfast: 80F.
Meals: From local caterers 70-850F.
Metro: Pont Marie, Cité, St Paul; RER St Michel-Notre Dame.
Bus routes: 67
Car park: Quai de l'Hôtel de Ville.

The Palm Game, an Italian game that became tennis, was all the rage in 1634. Louis XIII gave permission to develop the island on condition a palm game court was built. Plus ça change.

Map No: 4

Le Pavillon Bastille   ★ ★ ★
65 rue de Lyon
Paris
75012

Tel: (1)43 43 65 65
Fax: (1)43 43 96 52

Management: Michel Arnaud & Maguiña Ramilo.

Behind a fine 19th-century townhouse façade we were stunned to find a Post-Modernist interior. This hotel has been very deliberately created from nought, with no deviation from the basic themes of blue, yellow, horizontal music-score lines (opéra oblige) and arc-of-circle — the result is a sophisticated, pleasing designer triumph (his name is Heim). And, moreover, attention to guests is paramount. Surprisingly, you arrive through the front court with its lovely old fountain to find the door locked so staff come to you and carry your luggage. Each evening you are invited to a wine-tasting in the modern/baroque lobby among the columns, deep blue drapes, tall metal lamps, hanging "masks" from demolished 1700s corbels and blue and yellow leather chairs. Rooms are all similar with very self-conscious designer elements and lots of mirrors to make the best of small spaces, using the blue and yellow colours and the straight-line and curve shapes. The TV +minibar unit has a curved mirror on top with a vase of fresh (blue and yellow) flowers under an ultra-mod suspended fragment of light. Bedside lighting is perfect, general and dim, individual and adjustable. Bathrooms have carefully-laid blue and white tile patterns with marble tops, fluffy towels, bathrobes and real glasses. It is all virtually brand new and irreproachable. We thought we would breakfast in the vaulted cellar rather than the pretty but noisy courtyard, whatever the weather.

Rooms: 24 + 1 suite.
Price: S or D 955F; suite 1375F; inc minibar.
Breakfast: 80F buffet.
Meals: Light meals about 100F.
Metro: Bastille; RER Gare de Lyon.
Bus routes: 28 29 63 65 91
Car park: Opéra Bastille.

The golden genie on top of the bronze Bastille column is presumed to represent Liberty breaking her bonds and sowing the Light into a glorious future.

Map No: 4

  exc Amex

Hôtel de la Place des Vosges ★★

12 rue de Birague
Paris
75004

Tel: (1)42 72 60 46
Fax: (1)42 72 02 64

Management: Philippe Cros.

One of the smallest hotels in Paris, it probably has some of the smallest rooms too. Indeed, built at the same time as the eponymous Place des Vosges in whose amicably awesome shadow it stands, this simple and unpretentious hotel has kept its original layout. What you see and live in here is the scale of a successful mule-hirer's house in 17th-century Paris. The old-furnished, comfy and welcoming lobby/breakfast area, so hushed after the traffic on rue St Antoine, was where the mule master tied his mules in days of gentler transport (the rings are still there in the old stone walls). The great beams overhead supported the hay loft, then his living quarters and right at the top his stable boys' garrets. There is an air of relaxed hard work that has come down with the centuries. This implies time to chat with visitors and guide them on their day's programme. Above the ground floor, you must expect less space. The tiny staircase (the lift goes from 1st to 4th floors) precludes large bags as does the pretty minimal storage space in the rooms. Decor is as simple as the atmosphere, pink and beige, old-fashioned satiny bedcovers, tiny but perfectly adequate shower and bathrooms. But if you travel light, what a wonderful part of Paris to be in, rich in history and alive with real 1990s Parisians.

Rooms: 16 with bath or shower & wc.
Price: S 310-420F; D 440-460F.
Breakfast: 40F.
Meals: None.
Metro: Bastille; RER Châtelet-Les Halles.
Bus routes: 69 86
Car park: 16 rue St Antoine.

Theme for meditation: the vast beam in the lobby was growing in the soil of France when Charlemagne was crowned Holy Roman Emperor in 800AD.

Map No: 4

     Visa only

Hôtel Saint-Louis   ✱ ✱ ✱
75 rue Saint-Louis-en-l'Ile
Paris
75004

Tel: (1)46 34 04 80
Fax: (1)46 34 02 13

Management: Guy & Andrée Record.

The Ile Saint Louis is the most exclusive 17th-century village in Paris. It is now a listed monument in its entirety and a very special place to stay. The Records' house on the "high street" is intimate, friendly (many clients have become lifelong friends) and utterly relaxed. You can lounge comfortably in the front room, watching the world go by, talking to Guy or Andrée about local events or the stars they have received, admiring the antiques they have collected. The basement breakfast room has a splendid medieval dungeon atmosphere with a barred window for air (what a blessing) but no escape, running water (actually a stone fountainhead set into a wall), low arches and heavy little doors to hidden places. Bedrooms are decorated similarly throughout with a muted mushroom/mauve/pink base, soft pink and blue piqué bedcovers, plain blue curtains and cane furniture. There are elaborate gilt-framed mirrors, reading lights and beams (of course). Bathrooms are modern and lack no 3-star gadgets. None of the rooms is very large; some give more impression of space with two windows on a corner. As this really is an island there is blessedly little traffic noise at night. An additional charm is that there are no television sets.

Rooms: 21 with bath or shower.
Price: D 695F; T 795F.
Breakfast: 47F.
Meals: None.
Metro: Pont-Marie; RER Châtelet-Les Halles.
Bus routes: 67
Car park: Pont-Marie.

About 1360, a "trial by duel" took place here before King Charles V between a faithful, "orphaned" dog and its master's presumed murderer...who admitted his guilt.

 Visa only

Hôtel Saint-Louis Marais (ex-Célestins) **
1 rue Charles V
Paris
75004

Tel: (1)48 87 87 04
Fax: (1)48 87 33 26

Management: Guy & Andrée Record.

On the corner of two quiet streets a modest glazed front door opens onto a large, warmly vibrant lobby/lounge with old beams, stones and tiles, collector's bits (a medieval bishop and an 18th-century slave boy), rich woven curtains, tapestries and rugs. The reception is a normal desk so your first contact is as informal and relaxed as the hotel itself; the place oozes peace from its 300-year-old oaks. No television in bedrooms but addicts will find a television room in the basement, beside the vaulted breakfast room. No lift either but the stairwell is beautiful, the steps old stone with red carpet and an acanthus-pattern runner, ancient shotguns and an imitation Greek Venus in niches — it feels like a rather grand private house. The rooms are in keeping, with softly clothed walls and Chinese-inspired curtains and bedcovers or deeper-coloured walls and pastelly floral draperies. There are beams everywhere and the owners' passion for old cupboard doors is evident — they do finish a room most elegantly. All rooms are light and airy. Twin rooms are the most generous on space, singles are tight with all items (desktop, bedside shelves, lights) in miniature. Bathrooms vary in colour from white to very bright blue. It is all reassuringly human in scale, restful and exceptionally hospitable.

Rooms: 16 with bath or shower.
Price: S 515F; D 615F; T 715F.
Breakfast: 43F.
Meals: None.
Metro: Sully Morland; RER Gare de Lyon.
Bus routes: 86 87.
Car park: Pont Marie; rue St Antoine.

The scruffy but fascinating Hôtel Fieubet, quai des Célestins, is an extravaganza of baroque stonework — the figures seem about to climb off the walls. Admire it before it disintegrates.

(12)   **Map No:** 4

Sorbonne
•
Pantheon
•
St Séverin
•
St Julien le Pauvre
•
Cluny Museum
•
Rue Mouffetard
•
Institut du Monde Arabe

Latin Quarter

Grand Hôtel des Balcons **

3 rue Casimir Delavigne
Paris
75006

Tel: (1)46 34 78 50
Fax: (1)46 34 06 27

Management: Denise & Pierre Corroyer.

 Visa only

It is indeed greatly balconied, and moulded, and corniced! But it is the Art Nouveau interior that is the real delight. This is all Denise Corroyer's work. She took the original 1890s windows (don't miss the irises, lilies, tulips and twining bindweed on the staircase either) with their voluptuous curves and fresh vegetation and copied their designs onto the panelling, screening and lighting (amazing modern copies), even the shape of the window blinds. Having done the permanent parts, she now concentrates on great displays of pots and plants. There is a touch of humour too — a lifesize black servant boy sits smiling on a shelf; a touch of eroticism — a full-bodied Venus supervises the breakfast room; a sense of lightness and pleasure that the owners and staff communicate as effectively as their surroundings. They enjoy their clientele of Anglo-Saxons, Japanese (painters not businessmen), or antipodeans (athletes who dash off on tropical mornings to run in the Luxembourg lanes). Their rooms are excellent value for two stars. They are far from enormous but judicious designing of built-in table and shelf units helps; streetside rooms have, of course, balconies. At the back, you may be woken by the birds! The whole place is in prime condition (an eagle eye is kept and no damage left unrepaired for long), with firm beds, good bathrooms, simple but pleasant colours and materials — and a feast for breakfast.

Rooms: 55 with bath or shower.
Price: S 330-370F; D 420-475F; TR 545F.
Breakfast: 50F buffet including sausages, ham, eggs, cheese.
Meals: None.
Metro: Odéon; RER Luxembourg.
Bus routes: 24 63 86 87 96
Car park: Ecole de Médecine .

Despite modern cinematic deviations and the theatrical example just up the road, "odeon" ("odeum") in fact meant a hall for singing and other musical performances.

Map No: 4

 50F

Hôtel le Clos Médicis

* * *

56 rue Monsieur le Prince
Paris
75006

Tel: (1)43 29 10 80
Fax: (1)43 54 26 90

Management: Monsieur Beherec & Olivier Méallet.

With old stone walls and glazed frontage, the Clos Médicis still looks like the shop it (partly) was. Virtually rebuilt in 1994, the former narrow hotel entrance hall was given light and space by incorporating an old bookshop. As you come in from the excited boulevard St Michel, you see a fine stone pillar, are led past the old mirror towards the light of the quiet sunny patio and the reception, while being aware on your right of an attractive countersunk area with old beams, a welcoming (winter) fire and comfy armchairs. Gentle jazz can be heard. This place combines old and new, Parisian and provincial, most successfully. A "clos" is a vineyard — each room is named after a famous wine. Bathrooms are impeccably fitted — and the tiling has a Provençal feel. There are beams and pictures in antique frames throughout, coordinated "designer" materials, bold patterns and modern colours, wave-shaped bedheads and tall medieval-inspired lampshades, designed by the architect. Some rooms show a sober, masculine elegance; others have more floral tendencies. Room 46 has a Pluto-grey bathroom; No 65 is a nicely-arranged duplex; No 12 has a private terrace. Care has been taken to make noise a thing you leave out in the street. The fully soundproofed rooms are elegant, carefully designed, not always very big but extremely comfortable and the Beherec sense of hospitality is as tangible here as at the Neuville.

Rooms: 22 doubles, 16 twins.
Price: D 780-980F; DP 1200F.
Breakfast: 60F with fresh juice, cheese, hard-boiled eggs, fruit salad.
Meals: On request 100-180F.
Metro: Odéon; RER Luxembourg.
Bus routes: 21 38 82 84 85 89
Car park: Rue Soufflot.

It will astonish some to learn that the façade of the Cinéma 3 Luxembourg opposite is listed as an historical monument. You may now go back to gaze, perchance to admire...

Hôtel Esmeralda

4 rue Saint-Julien-le-Pauvre
Paris
75005

Tel: (1)43 54 19 20
Fax: (1)40 51 00 68

Management: Michèle Bruel.

You feel that the whole of Left Bank, artistic, eccentric Paris is concentrated here. Madame Bruel, sporting cigarette-holder and ethnic-weave jacket, has been a pillar of the impoverished intellectual traveller's cosmos for many years and will tell you her fascinating life story at the drop of a hat, show you her work (she is an artist herself), expect you to love her cats and damn all bureaucrats to eternal flames. The Esmeralda is old, very old, and dark and creaky and smelling of polish and dog. It is also noisy, on the edge of the pedestrian Latin Quarter, but what matter when you have Notre Dame on your left and St Julien le Pauvre, the oldest church in Paris, on your right? Up the very fine original (1640) staircase, along twisting sloping corridors to rooms that, however small, are also full of character, with florals and fireplaces, chandeliers and ancient bedheads. There are undoubtedly some nice antique pieces (an inlaid sideboard, ornate mirrors), including certain bits of wallpaper... All rooms are different, the largest look across the Seine to Notre Dame, the smallest are like cupboards, facilities are basic but perfectly adequate. Few concessions to modernity but massive quantities of atmosphere and encounters with famous names from showbiz if you're lucky(?). Book early — it is VERY popular.

Rooms: 19 with bath, shower or basin & wc.
Price: S 160F; D 320-490F.
Breakfast: 40F.
Meals: None.
Metro: St Michel; RER St Michel-Notre Dame.
Bus routes: 21 24 27 38 96
Car park: Notre Dame.

Your lady hostess (+ex-husband) relaunched the Bâteaux Mouches after the war with an old boat that she painted entirely by hand — "the only real one on the river".

Map No: 4

Hôtel Résidence les Gobelins   **
9 rue des Gobelins
Paris
75013

Tel: (1)47 07 26 90
Fax: (1)43 31 44 05

Management: Monsieur Poirier.

The street, the hotel, the owner are all as quiet and unassuming as each other — no need for double glazing. This was a neighbourhood of modest dwellings for people working at the great Gobelins tapestry workshops and was never very smart. But it is close to the bohemian rue Mouffetard with its little eating houses, lively market, mosque and left-wing culture. The lobby/lounge, with simple rattan furniture and thick floral cushions, and the airy breakfast room, decorated with much-loved black and white photographs of Paris and Parisians, lie round a small plant-filled courtyard with welcoming tables and chairs. The rooms are as simple as the rest and there is enough space. Nothing superfluous can be detected yet all the essentials are there, on a basic theme of pastel-coloured walls, white piqué or striped Indian cotton bedcovers, a writing table and chair and a decent cupboard. Some have been redecorated more recently than others, some wallpapers need redoing; Monsieur Poirier works his way round gradually and they will be seen to. All the rooms are quiet and light though party walls seemed rather thin. The gentle unobtrusive friendliness reminds the sensitive guest that this used to be a "pension de famille" — it has kept that incomparable sense of intimacy and understanding.

Rooms: 32 with bath or shower.
Price: S 365-395F; D 400-455F;
TR 585F.
Breakfast: 37F.
Meals: Delivered 50-150F.
Metro: Gobelins; RER Port Royal.
Bus routes: 27 47 83 91
Car park: Place d'Italie.

Gobelins is the great name of great French tapestries but the Gobelin brothers were in fact simple dyers and the streams here ran blood red from their labours.

 50F

 exc Diners

Hôtel Jardin de l'Odéon ⭐⭐⭐

7 rue Casimir Delavigne
Paris
75006

Tel: (1)46 34 23 90
Fax: (1)43 25 28 12

Management: Monsieur & Madame Mouton.

Art lovers abound in the Odéon neighbourhood. Monsieur Mouton is one of them. In his parents' time, half the lobby was his separate art gallery, started for the benefit of his many artist friends. We'd love to join in discussions about abstract v figurative at the bar here, under the attentive portrait of the pre-war barman. Still an enthusiastic member of the art world, your host displays his design talent in the overall Arts Deco style of his refurbished hotel and various fine details (the logotype is his as are the delightful fountain gracing the bamboo-filled patio and the black inlay pattern on bedheads and street-side windows). He inherited the breakfast-room chairs, chose the Mackintosh copies for the bedrooms and designed the rest of the furniture. Three colour schemes — blue, pink, yellow — prevail for the pastel-sponged walls and abstract-print curtains and covers in the cleancut, coolly uncluttered bedrooms. Bathrooms are white with a choice of three frieze motifs. Storage space is good behind mirrored sliding doors. The style is elegant and unfrilly, the beds have wood-slat bases and firm interior-sprung mattresses. Seven rooms, oh miracle, have private terraces with ivy growing up the trellises and views onto the patio or, on the top floor, out towards the neo-classical façade of the Odéon theatre. This hotel has lots of quiet space on the ground floor, average-sized and very pleasant rooms...and two lifts. Its young, relaxed owners are ever willing to help you arrange your days.

Rooms: 41 with bath or shower.
Price: S 406-606F; D 812-1012F;
TR 1018-1218F.
Breakfast: 50F.
Meals: None.
Metro: Odéon; RER Luxembourg.
Bus routes: 58 63 70 86 87 96
Car park: Ecole de Médecine.

Map No: 4

Gérard Mulot, one of the best pastry shops in Paris with a tiny tea room, is just down the road on the corner of rue de Seine and rue Lobineau.

Hôtel de Notre Dame ★ ★ ★

19 rue Maître Albert
Paris
75005

Tel: (1)43 26 79 00
Fax: (1)46 33 50 11

Management: Monsieur Fouhety.

  exc Diners

On a quiet little street off the embankment in one of the oldest parts of Paris, a most attractive red-framed glass frontage opens onto a large lobby decorated with a magnificent tapestry, bits of antiquity, deep armchairs and huge bunches of flowers. The image of openness is confirmed — these people seem genuinely to like people. Beyond the lobby there is a small inviting bar and breakfast area. If the age of the building (1600s) is evident in the convolutions of the corridors, contemporary style dictates their smart black "dados" with tan or sea-green uppers. Guestrooms also show the mix of old and new. There are beams and exposed stones, some of them enormous, and views of Notre Dame from the higher floors, though the windows are much smaller here than on the first floor. Most rooms have a porch-like entrance created by a large curvy "shelf" built below ceiling level to carry the discreet spotlights. The made-to-measure desk/table units reflect this design. Upholstery is warm and light with soft-coloured suede or small-flowered cotton walls, Pierre Frey curtains and bedcovers in gentle checks or pastel florals. We liked the translucent Japanese screen doors to bathrooms — an excellent idea for small layouts; not all baths are full size. Some details need refreshing — refreshment is planned. The black eunuch portrayed as Marie-Antoinette's feathered fan bearer lived here...

Rooms: 34 with bath (exc 1 with shower).
Price: D 690F; T 750F.
Breakfast: 40F.
Meals: None.
Metro: Maubert Mutualité; RER St Michel-Notre Dame.
Bus routes: 47 63 86 87
Car park: La Grange.

On the square at the end of the road, two shops: the only place in Paris specialising in patchwork and a knowledgeable dealer in Native American art and literature.

Map No: 4

Le Notre-Dame Hôtel ★★★

1 quai Saint Michel
Paris
75005

Tel: (1)43 54 20 43
Fax: (1)43 26 61 75

Management: Jacques Rols.

Up a mirrored staircase from the noisy embankment you will find the reception and an attractive beamed bar on the first floor offering vast views of Notre Dame, the Seine, the booksellers' stands and crowds of students and tourists — this hotel is at the hub of the Latin Quarter. Yet the staff will quickly make you feel you belong here. As in a dream, you can study the cathedral's medieval stone wonders from your bedroom window. The window is fully soundproofed for a peaceful sleep (though rooms ending in 5 give onto a quiet if dingy courtyard). The rooms are not large but uncluttered and full of light from the river, with cane or modern-style white lacquer/silver trim made-to-measure furniture, deep raspberry or pale mushroom cloth on walls, gentle carpets, soft print draperies and nice china lamps. The corner rooms (ending in 2) have brilliant round-the-corner views. The duplex rooms are striking. You reach them from a landing with a delightful timber frame + skylight detail. No 63 has an elegant little red sitting room with strong abstract upholstery on the convertible sofa, a gold plush French armchair, a small antique desk, an equally small window and loads of atmosphere; up tiny stairs (do mind your head) to a sleeping area with full view of Notre Dame from the velux window. The well-designed bathrooms are fashionably marbled or pin-stripe-tiled.

Rooms: 26 with shower or bath.
Price: S/D 590-790F; DP 1050F.
Breakfast: 40F.
Meals: None.
Metro: St Michel; RER St Michel-Notre Dame.
Bus routes: 24 47
Car park: Notre Dame.

Run out of bedtime reading? George Whitman's world-famous "Shakespeare & Co" new and secondhand English-language bookshop is just down the road.

Map No: 4

Port-Royal Hôtel *
8 boulevard de Port-Royal
Paris
75005

Tel: (1)43 31 70 06
Fax: (1)43 31 33 67

Management: Thierry Giraud.

The Giraud family have been running this super-simple one-star hotel for 64 years and still do it with conscientious enjoyment. It reminds me of those lucky finds as a student in pricey Paris : clean, friendly, utterly unpretentious and brilliantly cheap. If you are alone and broke and don't mind the loo down the passage (the more expensive rooms have their own), base yourself here, just minutes from the trendy rue Mouffetard with its lively street market and the ancient St Médard church (the only one where you can receive absolution for cannibalism) and a short walk from the Latin Quarter. The boulevard is perfectly leafily Parisian (streetside rooms have double glazing), the hotel has a dear little inner patio where, in summer, a plain and nourishing breakfast amongst the plants will set you on your way while the Girauds will help you all they can in planning your day. This is also one of the hotels with more French than foreign guests, so you could use this time to practise your French. Most of the rooms are fairly small — but this is true all over Paris — the furnishing basic and the beds adequate. There is nothing extravagant, there is no lift, rooms have neither telephone nor television and walls are fairly thin but it is all scrupulously clean and they are SUCH NICE PEOPLE. Wonderful value.

Rooms: 45 with washbasin only or shower or bath & wc.
Price: S 150-190F; D 190-280F.
Breakfast: 24F.
Meals: None.
Metro: Gobelins; RER Gare d'Austerlitz.
Bus routes: 27 47 83 91
Car park: Patriarche.

So close to the Santé prison, the hotel was used overnight by priest and executioner before their 5am (public) appointments with Mme Guillotine and her unhappy prey.

Map No: 4

Hôtel Saint-Paul Rive Gauche   ★ ★ ★

43 rue Monsieur le Prince
Paris
75006

Tel: (1)43 26 98 64
Fax: (1)46 34 58 60

Management: Marianne Hawkins.

The Franco-British Hawkins family have been running hotels for four generations — and loving it. Their pleasure is evident from the cared-for ivy on the front wall to the Indian rugs strewn everywhere, from the decorative cast-iron firebacks (Madame's passion) to the two trees in the tiny patio that spread magnificently outside the upper windows. The communal areas are large and generous, marrying French elegance with English comfort plus Perkins, the black and white cat. He is easy about visitors; the staff are lively, welcoming and... relaxed. Bedrooms vary in size and some are due for renovation. Bathrooms are red, pink or ginger marble and modern. There are beams and timbers, views of the Sorbonne and Pantheon domes (from top-floor suites), high ceilings (the lower your floor, the higher your ceiling) and 17th-century furniture. These elements are set off by strong colours — deep blue, yellow or raspberry-fool walls with contrasted curtains and bedcovers — a tapestry-upholstered chair, a brass bed, a carved bed, a canopied bed. You feel the comfort is designed for you and you are meant to be here. Rooms at the back overlook the hotel's fine trees and the playground and greenhouse of the Lycée St Louis. Some of the Saint Paul's window boxes grow herbs and tomatoes as well as flowers.

Rooms: 31 (inc 2 suites & 1 duplex) with bath or shower.
Price: S 585-665F; D 665-965F; ST 965-1185F.
Breakfast: 48F; 68F with eggs.
Meals: Light meals on request 80-150F.
Metro: Odéon; RER Luxembourg.
Bus routes: 38 63 82 85 86 87 95 96
Car park: Ecole de Médecine.

Parts of King Philippe Auguste's vast city walls can be seen here. We know him as the conqueror of bad King John "Lackland" of England who lost Normandy to him in 1204.

St Germain des Prés – Orsay

Ouï-dire

Hearsay

Temps mort

Slack time/period

Hôtel de Beaune ★★

29 rue de Beaune
Paris
75007

Tel: (1)42 61 24 89
Fax: (1)49 27 02 12

Management: Madame Chelali.

You are of course in "Antique-dealers' Zone" here, and you might well think No 29 is not an hotel but another antique shop with its oh-so-discreet brass nameplate on an old-fashioned frontage and just two fine Moorish-style pots in the window. Uncluttered is the theme throughout. Another leitmotiv is American film stars. The third is pink. You first meet pink in the reception desk and then in every bedroom and bathroom. The lobby is also gently decorated with original watercolours hung for a few months then changed, "to give another artist a turn", cane-and-cushioned armchairs and a view down the corridor towards Andy Warhol's Marilyn Monroe. Four of her adorn the wall of the breakfast room/bar which is furnished with bistro tables and chairs, more cane armchairs, indoor plants and... a large television. The bedrooms are all just as simple. Jimmy's Den in memory of James Dean and Marilyn's room have more pictures than most. Each has one bistro table and two chairs, plain cloth-hung walls, white bedcovers and curtains and a pink-tiled shower or bathroom with a pretty engraved mirror. The tiling is sometimes in need of renovation, the paintwork a little worn here and there, but the Beaune is still excellent value in this smartest of Left Bank neighbourhoods where artists and stars congregate. It is small, quiet, unpretentious and Madame Chelali just as quietly welcoming and helpful.

Rooms: 18 + 1 mini-suite, with bath or shower & wc
Price: ST 850F; D 450-570F; S 430-450F.
Breakfast: 40F included.
Meals: Light meals on request 50-150F.
Metro: St Germain-des-Prés; RER Musée d'Orsay.
Bus routes: 24 27 39 48 63 68 69 70 87 95
Car park: Montalembert.

It is not the city of fine Burgundy that is commemorated here but the minor 17th-century astronomer-mathematician who gave his name to a geometry problem.

Map No: 4

50F

Hôtel Bersoly's Saint Germain***

28 rue de Lille
Paris
75007

Tel: (1)42 60 73 79
Fax: (1)49 27 05 55

Management: Monsieur & Mademoiselle Carbonnaux.

Closed in August. Guests are welcomed here as members of the family. How could they be otherwise in such a tiny, intimate house? Sylvie Carbonnaux is charming and unflappable. Her father, with a fine head of hair as white as his Westie's fur, is a firm and gentle presence. Built in the 1600s as a convent, the house has the patina of a genuine antique, from the beautiful irregular paving stones of the lobby to the slim elegance of the listed banisters. Rather than the slightly reluctant lift, take the stairs and enjoy the Impressionist copies (old friends?) in heavy frames on the landings. The rooms, each named for and hung with a painter's work, recall the original cell dimensions imposed upon the nuns — they are very small, with old beams and large modern ceiling fans. Bathrooms are practical and pretty, each has a different tiling motif. Furnishings are soft shades of pink and yellow or, unexpectedly, large floral designs that set off the old wardrobes and tables. A suite of 2 communicating rooms can be created on each floor. Top-floor rooms have sloping ceilings and more space (room for a couple of armchairs); "Pissaro's" bath sits inside the timber frame! and "Degas'" bathroom is up a private stair. On the ground floor, "Picasso" is reached through its own tiny courtyard with garden furniture and a great sense of privacy. To reach the finely vaulted breakfast rooms in the basement you go past the small attractive bar and look forward to your evening aperitif.

Rooms: 16 with shower or bath.
Price: 580-680F.
Breakfast: 50F + à la carte.
Meals: Caterer lunch 60-150F.
Metro: St Germain des Prés, Rue du Bac; RER Musée d'Orsay.
Bus routes: 24 27 39 48 63 68 69 86 87 95
Car park: Hotel or Montalembert

The brave citizens of Lille are commemorated here for resisting the Austrians in 1792 when all the crowned heads of Europe ganged up on the French Revolution.

Map No: 4

Hôtel Bourgogne et Montana ***
3 rue de Bourgogne
Paris
75007

Tel: (1)45 51 20 22
Fax: (1)45 56 11 98

Management: Madame Monney.

The district is very smart with important people (like MPs) dashing about in the daytime but as soon as you enter the also-smart Bourgogne you feel a delicious relief — these hotel people only take themselves half seriously, the half required to do their job properly. The other half is all light-hearted self-deprecatory attentive welcome. The MP theme is used throughout, with wicked cartoon portraits of real individuals... from an earlier generation. We like this combination of efficiency and wit — the French at their best. Beyond the lobby is the rotunda with its pink pilasters and mirrors and unreal roundness — the inner well above it, round to the sky, is due to be trellissed and ivied — the dark-panelled, leather-chaired meeting/sitting room and the deeply tempting breakfast room, full of light and the most sinful buffet (included in the price). The lift is a wonder of pre-war panels and ironwork. From the upper floors you see Paris laid out: the National Assembly, Concorde, Madeleine... It IS a luxy hotel, especially the suites and "superior" rooms which have space and antique furniture, lovely china lamps, thick quilted upholstery, dimmer switches for individual reading lights and some (Nos 57 and 67) extraordinary bathrooms. But the staff are charming and the smaller (cheaper) rooms are still extremely comfortable, with the same harmonious use of mix'n match colours and patterns, perfectly good marble and tile bathrooms and...that feast for breakfast. If full, try the Madison.

Rooms: 34 with bath or shower.
Price: S 580-1360F; D 870-1420F.
Breakfast: Included.
Meals: From caterer 100-300F.
Metro: Assemblée Nationale,
Invalides(+RER+ Air France bus).
Bus routes: 93 83 63.
Car park: Invalides.

No 9 belonged to Lucien Bonaparte (Nap's brother) whose mistress lived there; but he lived at 9 rue St Dominique so had a tunnel built between the two mansions...easy.

Hôtel du Globe ★★

15 rue des Quatre-Vents
Paris
75006

Tel: (1)46 33 62 69
Fax: (1)43 26 35 50

Management: Simonne Ressier.

Closed in August. Miniature is the word, for the hotel itself, the rooms, the staircase, the storage — your luggage will need to be pretty miniature too — but huge are the hearts of the small team who run it. They simply adore their little hostelry. We certainly found it instantly lovable. If you greet the iron man properly, walk up the stairs (there is no lift) without banging your nose on your own reflection or tripping over the thick knobbly carpet, and stop on the first landing you will find the discreet "reception" in a sitting room full of furniture and papers and no office equipment at all…You are in someone's house and they welcome you with a smile rather than a form to fill in. All the bedcovers are grandmotherly crochet, there are beams and old stones and four-posters, pink rooms and yellow rooms with little carved gueridon tables, tiny folding writing tables, rich-framed mirrors and dozens more personal bits and pieces. No two rooms are alike. The smallest have shower and basin and loo neatly hidden behind folding doors that would be plain off-the-peg cupboard doors if they weren't hand-painted by a skilful artist. The rooms with bathrooms are larger — one on the ground floor has its own tiny patio — and wherever you sleep you also have your breakfast as there is no breakfast room. For character, charm and warmth of welcome, the Globe is hard to beat. (But do take your earplugs in case of a streetside (disco-side) room.)

Rooms: 15 rooms with bath or shower.
Price: S/D 330-440F; child's bed 50F.
Breakfast: 40F.
Meals: None.
Metro: Odéon; RER Cluny-La Sorbonne.
Bus routes: 86 87
Car park: St Sulpice.

Map No: 4

In the 17th century, the four winds blew to the four corners of the earth from the round cheeks and delicious lips of four cherubs — on a shop sign.

50F

Hôtel Lenox Saint-Germain   ★★★

9 rue de l'Université
Paris
75007

Tel: (1)42 96 10 95
Fax: (1)42 61 52 83

Management: Emmanuel Destouches.

As at the Montparnasse Lenox, the airy, welcoming bar and its clients lend tremendous atmosphere to this hotel. It is used by the Gallimard publishing team for drinks after work, by film stars for interviews with journalists and fights with partners, by writers for long literary arguments — in short, it is utterly St Germain des Prés and great fun. Ask Wojtek the photographer/barman to tell you all the stories. If you are coming to sleep only, you enter from a quiet street through great blue wooden doors into a large mirrored hall with elegant sitting spaces around the fireplace. The staff are exceptionally friendly and you will feel immediately welcome. There are false duplexes and real ones, large rooms and (much) smaller ones. All are different, all have the large hallmark period mirror that the owners take such trouble finding and often another nice piece of furniture, though some bedheads and table tops are more modern and synthetic, some "armoires" are new-into-old. Colour schemes are mostly muted. Rooms on the little rue du Pré aux Clercs are quieter than the others; some have the added luxury of a balcony (or two), while those on lower floors have higher moulded ceilings. We really liked the corner rooms with two windows and lots of light, even if the "spear" curtain rails were a little intimidating. Bathrooms are good and extra shelving for pots and paints is provided by little trolleys. An excellent place to make you feel you belong in St Germain.

Rooms: 34 with shower or bath.
Price: D 590-830F; DP 960F.
Breakfast: 45F.
Meals: On request 60-150F.
Metro: St Germain des Prés; RER Orsay.
Bus routes: 63 68 69 83 94
Car park: Montalembert.

The tramp hero of "Les Amants du Pont Neuf" spent a month in the Best Room here while filming but was forbidden to wash for the sake of more authentic tramphood.

Map No: 4

Hôtel Louis II   ★ ★ ★
2 rue Saint-Sulpice
Paris
75006

Tel: (1)46 33 13 80
Fax: (1)46 33 17 29

Management: Madame Siozade.

At the top of this 18th-century corner building you can sleep under the ancient sloping roof timbers in one of two long flower-papered triple rooms (these are the two air-conditioned rooms of the Louis II) where crochet bed and table coverings are so fitting. In one there is an old rustic "armoire", in the other a 1920s free-standing full-length oval mirror. One bathroom has brass taps and a yellow cockle-shell basin, the other has an oval bath and burnished copper fittings. The decorator's imagination has been unleashed throughout this charming house, often to dramatic effect (one wc has deep pink satin bamboo wallpaper), so that even the smallest rooms (some are very tight with little storage space) have huge personality. Two rooms have dazzling wraparound trompe l'oeil pictures (by the artist who painted the lift doors) set into the timber frame (the wall-mounted safe becomes a shelf for a great vase of flowers, for example). Every room is different, sheets are floral, bath/ shower rooms are small but fully equipped. Come down in the morning to revel in the slightly worn elegance of the sitting/breakfast room. It is large, lit from two sides and has a fanning beam structure to carry the ceiling round the corner. Gilt-framed mirrors add to the sense of movement and some fine antique pieces and candelabras complete the picture. As at the nearby Globe (under the same management), you will be enthusiastically welcomed and properly cared for.

Rooms: 22 with bath or shower.
Price: S/D 560-720F; TR 880F; child under 5 free.
Breakfast: 44F.
Meals: None.
Metro: Odéon; RER St Michel-Notre Dame.
Bus routes: 63 87 86 96 58 70.
Car park: St Sulpice.

Louis II was the great 17th-century Bourbon Prince de Condé who rebelled against Louis XIV the child king and fought brilliantly for Louis XIV the Sun King.

Le Madison

⋆ ⋆ ⋆

143 boulevard Saint-Germain
Paris
75006

Tel: (1)40 51 60 00
Fax: (1)40 51 60 01

Management: Madame Burkard.

St Germain, St Germain...the bar of the Madison is one of the places one may be seen — so you can imagine the trendy atmosphere that greets you as you walk in. The staff have the appropriate mix of class and 1990s cheerfulness. The hotel is in a tree-lined square, set just back from the boulevard and right opposite the vastly celebrated Deux Magots café. The public rooms are big and attractive (and about to be completely refurbished). The solemn salon, with tapestry, pillars and plush sofas, will reflect your discreet business meeting in many silent mirrors. In light contrast, beyond the bar with its winter log fires and powerful cockerel-astride-a-wheatsheaf in "porcelaine de Saxe", the breakfast room will receive you gently under its triptych of original 18th-century screens where the grand spread on its fine old sideboard cannot fail to seduce you. Bedrooms are relatively small after these great spaces and very functionally furnished, though renovation is under way and brighter, more contemporary ideas are being used. We liked the larger, double-windowed rooms over the boulevard. No 14 has blue and beige and green colours with a fine dark green china lamp and shade on a nice old desk and the bathroom is deep red marble. Next door is a smaller room that some clients love — deep raspberry walls, very bright yellow bedcovers and curtains, royal blue lamp and chair...vital and provocative to the eye! If full, try the Bourgogne.

Rooms: 55 with bath or shower.
Price: S 760-1262F; D 1015-1500F.
Breakfast: Included.
Meals: From caterer 100-300F.
Metro: St Germain des Prés; RER Châtelet-Les Halles.
Bus routes: 86 48 95 87
Car park: St Germain des Prés.

Nowadays, some come to be anonymous for deep deals they can't do at the Ritz but in an earlier simpler life the Madison housed Camus while he wrote "L'Etranger".

Map No: 4

Hôtel de Nesle

7 rue de Nesle
Paris
75006

Tel: (1)43 54 62 41

Management: Madame Busillet & David Busillet.

In a tiny street between Odéon and Seine, there is no other hotel like it and no other owner like Madame Renée, as everyone calls the good-looking matron who rules the Nesle with voice, gesture and bonhomie. With its plain furniture and bunches of dried flowers, the reception/sitting/breakfast room communicates the generally carefree atmosphere. Then, first floor, first surprise : a real garden, with roses, apricot trees, a pond and two aggressive ducks (sticks beside the door for your protection). Half the rooms give onto the garden. The second surprise is in your room: the walls carry bright, lively frescoes designed to initiate foreigners into the history of Paris and France. Try "Afrique" for French explorers, mosquito-netted bed and genuine African objects, "Sahara" for a private open patio with a genuine (miniature) hammam or "Ancienne", the last pre-70s room, for old photographs, lace mats and Toile de Jouy. The Nesle, a favourite with backpackers, struggling academics and those who travel light, is spotlessly clean and has good firm mattresses. BUT, even if the price suits your pocket and the old beams please your eye, you may decide the facilities and services are too scant for your comfort — virtually no storage or hanging space, one wc per 4 rooms (à la turque on the 5th floor) and advance booking is not allowed. Ring or come in the morning for the evening...and enjoy the deliciously warm friendliness of the place.

Rooms: 20 with washbasin or shower, all sharing wc.
Price: Inc breakfast: S 210F; D 270F; D with shower 360F.
Breakfast: 25F included.
Meals: None.
Metro: Odéon; RER St Michel-Notre Dame.
Bus routes: 58 63 70 86 87 96
Car park: Rue Mazarine.

The Tower of Nesle was (in)famous for housing princesses who seduced and "used" handsome young men then threw them into the river to conceal their depravities.

Hôtel le Régent
***

61 rue Dauphine
Paris
75006

Tel: (1)46 34 59 80
Fax: (1)40 51 05 07

Management: Madame Martin.

The spaces are small but the designer has used his art to prove that space is a mental construct. We admire his talent. He uses wood, cloth, mirrors and light to shape, stretch and enhance his volumes. No room for canopies over beds? The idea will be created in two dimensions on the wall. The "attic" feels cramped with its sloping ceiling? We'll underline it with fine polished wooden slats and turn it into a feature. Bedcovers look heavy? We'll design pretty, thin quilts for each room. One has two balconies onto Notre Dame, geraniums galore, ochre and blue ethnic-style upholstery, a matching bathroom. The three upper floors all have daring colour schemes and brilliant tiled bathrooms. Pleasing contrasts are achieved with Louis XV gilt-framed mirrors in these designer surroundings. Observe the fine 1730s façade and you will see why the three lower floors with their high moulded windows are called "noble" and demand more traditional treatment. Some are quite large, their fabulously tall elegant windows draped with thick swagged curtains, the furniture is period, the general atmosphere more sober. All rooms have a neat system of built-in cupboards and niches concealing televisions and minibars. The lobby recalls the hotel's age and name with genuine old paintings in heavy frames, richly-upholstered armchairs, columns and painted beams. Madame Martin and her staff run the Régent with friendly humour and Parisian dynamism — a great combination.

Rooms: 25 with bath or shower.
Price: 750F (smaller) & 950F (larger).
Breakfast: 55F with fresh orange juice.
Meals: None.
Metro: Odéon; RER St Michel-Notre Dame.
Bus routes: 27 58 63 70 86 87
Car park: Rue Mazarine.

The proprietor also owns the desperately famous Deux Magots café so you can buy your tea tin, cup or saucer here without actually having tea "over there"...

Map No: 4

 Visa

Hôtel Saint-André-des-Arts   *** ***

66 rue Saint-André-des-Arts
Paris
75006

Tel: (1)43 26 96 16
Fax: (1)43 29 73 34

Management: Monsieur Legoubin.

The old shop-front of this supremely relaxed, welcoming and low-cost hotel right beside the bustling Place St André-des-Arts has been known and loved by (mostly foreign) academics and intellectuals for years. They push the door onto a home from home to be greeted by a row of old choir stalls set on a 19th-century tiled floor, a timber frame surrounding a listed staircase and a former philosphy teacher. He much prefers running an hotel: the students come of their own accord and are HAPPY to talk "philo"...in all simplicity. The neighbourhood is lively, the music sometimes noisy and nocturnal, the atmosphere stimulating. Monsieur Legoubin's rooms all have "en-suite bathrooms", some are free-standing, all-in-one moulded cabins, all are perfectly adequate. The ceilings are sometimes immensely high with fine great windows to match, beams, timbers, old stone walls — all the signs of great age and lasting quality. The decor is simple too. Japanese grass paper in various shades on the walls, "ethnic" print curtains, practical basic furniture. In the corridors the walls are covered with coconut matting — an original and successful way of disguising irregularities with a natural material — but no effort is made to hide their twists and turns; they reveal the way the building was, and still is, articulated round the courtyard. One room is even reached by crossing a balcony. If you feel you would like to join this happy band, book early — it's often full.

Rooms: 34 with bath or shower & wc.
Price: D426-456F; S 298-333F.
Breakfast: Included in price.
Meals: None.
Metro: Odéon; RER St Michel-Notre Dame.
Bus routes: 63 70 86 87 96
Car park: Rue Mazarine.

The "arty" name may seem appropriate but it is actually a deformation of the more warlike "arc": people here made and sold bows and arrows in the 13th century.

Map No: 4

Hôtel de Saint-Germain ★ ★

50 rue du Four
Paris
75006

Tel: (1)45 48 91 64
Fax: (1)45 48 46 22

Management: Guy Lasalle.

The front door is sheer delight: arched windows in an old blue frame flanked by carved stone pilasters, capitals and lintel and topped by an iron-and-glass canopy. The image of the building's century-old beginnings. The lobby is small but mirrors, plants and friendly receptionists quickly calm you as you come in off the busy street. Age contributes to the peace. You can imagine yourself back in the village that was St Germain-des-Prés (in-the-fields, like London's St Martin's) 200/300 years ago... though the bathrooms are perfectly modern. The decoration speaks of two recent periods which cohabit comfortably. The top three floors, renovated in 1994 by the woman owner, have Laura Ashley wallpaper, a ceiling frieze, floral curtains and generally soft colours. The lower three floors have been redecorated by Guy Lasalle since he took over and you recognize a definitely masculine touch in the strong colours (vibrant combinations of blue, yellow and red — but not all at once!) and checks or large prints. He admits to a definite taste for blue. With simple polished pine furniture, sponge-painted walls and newly-tiled bathrooms, the effect is tonic. The rooms may be small (as is the basement breakfast room, and rather stuffy) with limited storage but this is a good-value spotlessly clean 2-star hotel with atmosphere, every modern comfort and a sincere welcome in occasionally supercilious St Germain-des-Prés.

Rooms: 30 with bath or shower.
Price: S 420-585F; D 595-695F.
Breakfast: 45F.
Meals: None.
Metro: St Germain des Prés; RER St Michel-Notre Dame.
Bus routes: 39 48 63 69 70 86 95 96
Car park: St Germain des Prés.

Poilane, the baker who astonishingly converted St Germain, Paris and France from white baguette to rough rye bread, has his shop in rue du Cherche-Midi, beyond the great bronze centaur.

Map No: 4

exc Diners

Hôtel de l'Université ★ ★ ★
22 rue de l'Université
Paris
75007

Tel: (1)42 61 09 39
Fax: (1)42 60 40 84

Management: Madame Bergmann & Monsieur Teissedre.

Oh! the luxury of space where a square metre is worth its weight in gold, the double-doored entrance, the vista through to the green patio, the split-level sitting rooms, the wide shallow staircase leading naturally to large, high-ceilinged bedrooms. And decorated like a grand embracing home with items that Madame Bergmann has ferretted out in flea markets and antique shops over the years: they fit so well. There are tapestries (or bits of) just in the right place, old prints in old frames ("Authentic or not at all — don't hold with copies" she says), wooden statues, pieces of furniture from all periods. The breakfast room gives onto the leafy patio. You eat at a long marble bistro table, seated on a fine long black velvet bench — or chez vous under the honeysuckle if you have taken one of the stunning terrace rooms. The other rooms are mostly just as generous (the singles would be instantly turned into doubles in many other hotels) with writing table, armchairs or sofa and white bedcovers that don't steal your attention away from the best pieces. Some have the original 18th-century panelling and built-in cupboards. All have good bathrooms, lots of marble and the right accessories. But enjoy the views too : over the Ministry of Commerce with its huge neo-classical portico and the Ecole Nationale d'Administration, academic cradle of great careers — innumerable senior civil servants, ministers and even Presidents of the Republic.

Rooms: 15 doubles; 10 singles; 2 with terrace; all with bath or shower.
Price: S 600-700F; D 800-900F; terrace rooms 1200-1300F.
Breakfast: 45F.
Meals: Light meals 50-100F.
Metro: St Germain des Prés; RER Musée d'Orsay.
Bus routes: 24 27 39 48 63 68 69 70 87 95
Car park: Montalembert.

At 218 bd St Germain is a tiny shop, in the Gély family since 1834, stuffed with canes and umbrellas, frequented by many of the Great and Good of France; a small marvel.

Map No: 4

Montparnasse – Luxembourg

Saillir

Project; stick out

Elle a fondu dans ses bras

She melted in his arms

Hôtel Acacias Saint-Germain ★★★

151 bis rue de Rennes
Paris
75006

Tel: (1)45 48 97 38
Fax: (1)45 44 63 57

Management: Cécile Ranchain-Siraut.

As you push the glass doors beyond the great wrought-iron gates, you leave the noise and fumes of bustling rue de Rennes and walk into a flower-filled entrance hall where your super-dynamic hostess, or one of her delightful receptionists, will greet you with enthusiasm, only too happy to help you organise your stay in Paris or further afield. Behind the low desk which makes the room feel like her own study, you can glimpse the little green courtyard where it is so tempting to take a cool evening drink in the summer or even swelter-proof breakfast when Paris pulls out all her tropical stops. Bedrooms and communal spaces are fairly small — but as ever, this is the heart of Paris and each square metre is at a premium. The basement breakfast room felt close and rather airless despite its light bright contemporary furnishings and lighting. However, renovations are constantly under way and this will be dealt with as well as the marbling of the bathrooms...The rooms are plainly furnished with modern functional units or contemporary scrubbed pine, plain walls, nice matching prints for covers and curtains and a sense of softness. They are mostly full of light — the higher the lighter of course — and have very good bedding. The greatest virtue here is attentive service and care for the individual.

Rooms: 41 with bath or shower.
Price: D/T 380-800F;
TR 600-1130F.
Breakfast: 40F.
Meals: Simple hotel meals or caterer deliveries.
Metro: Montparnasse; RER Port Royal.
Bus routes: 48 94 95 96
Car park: Montparnasse.

Next door, from 1856 to 1876, stood a temporary church built of red pine that was nicknamed Our Lady of the Planks because it was such a tatty load of consecrated old wood.

Map No: 4

Hôtel l'Aiglon * * *

232 boulevard Raspail
Paris
75014

Tel: (1)43 20 82 42
Fax: (1)43 20 98 72

Management: Jacques Rols.

Built over a smart brasserie, the Aiglon is a 3-star plus, its imperial eagle much exploited: Empire furniture, even an Empire lift, beside which trickles the stream of a delicious little rockery. In the Empire bar, leather "books" hide bottles and glasses while yellow plush armchairs offer gentle rest. The next delight is the large, light mahogany-panelled breakfast room over the leafy boulevard. Corridors are smartly red-clothed and each floor has a "public" wc — a rare commodity. All rooms have a lobby, walk-in cupboard and furniture made for the Aiglon (beds, chairs, chests of drawers-cum-minibar cover-ups); almost all are large for Paris and supremely restful. Walls are yellow or green cloth where furnishings are green and yellow, deep beige where muted multi-coloured prints reign; carpets are soft grey and brown, fine table lamps by Drimmer and watercolours add grace, firm new mattresses guarantee comfort. Bathrooms are well-equipped: even the small shower-rooms have proper-sized cabins, their light tiling set off by delicate friezes. All rooms give onto sycamore or acacia-lined avenues whence most traffic disappears at night, and some look over the green peace of Montparnasse cemetery. The deluxe apartment is "superbly appointed" (the minibar has little columns) and imperially vast. But the welcome is by no means haughtily Empire or powerfully Napoleonic. People stay for weeks, come again and are treated like old friends.

Rooms: 38 + 9 suites.
Price: S (shower) 480F; D 550-710F; ST 990F for 2; ST de luxe 1450F for 1-4.
Breakfast: 35F.
Meals: None.
Metro: Raspail; RER & Orly Bus: Denfert Rochereau.
Bus routes: 68 91
Car park: Hotel or Edgar Quinet.

Napoleon's son and heir, nicknamed the "Little Eagle", died in exile at 21 and never carried the Imperial insignia. The previous owner of the hotel was an ardent fan of Napoleon.

Map No: 4

L'Atelier Montparnasse ✳ ✳ ✳

49 rue Vavin
Paris
75006

Tel: (1)46 33 60 00
Fax: (1)40 51 04 21

Management: Marie-José Tible.

It is tiny, and fun, and utterly Montparnasse as we imagine it was in its heyday. The painter reigns supreme here. The lobby, large and embracing with a gripping mosaic floor (you can't take your eyes off it), contains easels and 20th-century paintings and has a generally 1930s feel about it. It is light and open and the relaxed and friendly owner is appropriately dressed in arty black. She occasionally organises exhibitions with private views in her hotel — to which current guests are naturally invited. But as I said, it is tiny. Three rooms per floor, the narrowest-gauge spiral staircase you have ever seen in a Paris building (there is a lift, of course), tiny landings, limited storage space...but complete soundproofing and masses of soul. Plus those extraordinary bathrooms. Every single one has a mosaic reproduction of a famous modern painting. Take your bath under the eyes of two dusky Gauguin women, snuggle right up to a Modigliani as you shower. And you will find your room extremely cosy if sometimes on the small side. The largest are the two sixth-floor rooms, "Fujita" being a double room with sitting area (and convertibla sofa), two windows, gentle Regency stripe curtains and lots of light. The beds are excellent, the kitschily absurd bedside lights are offset by sober still lifes, very unfussy dried flower bits and clean-lined bedheads. Definitely a special hotel near some of the places where one can really allow oneself to be seen.

Rooms: 17 with bath or shower.
Price: S 600F; D 700F; T 750F.
Breakfast: 40F.
Meals: From caterer 50-250F.
Metro: Vavin; RER Port Royal.
Bus routes: 83 91
Car park: Montparnasse.

Note that the famous cafés — Dôme, Select, Coupole — are more likely to provide a glimpse of artistic and literary luminaries at lunchtime than in the evening.

Hôtel de Bretagne-Montparnasse ***
33 rue Raymond-Losserand
Paris
75014

Tel: (1) 45 38 52 59
Fax: (1) 45 38 50 39

Management: Jean-Luc Houdré.

Tucked away among a jumble of streets (wonderful for walking, discovering, peeking into hidden courtyards) behind Montparnasse, the Bretagne was rebuilt rather than renovated in 1990 and has put aside any memories of its 19th-century past. It is functional, comfortable, bright and relaxed; there are boxes of geraniums at 20-odd windows, and the welcome you receive is enthusiastic. Jean-Luc Houdré leaves his mark on other details too. The continental breakfast buffet is excellent value with no limit on quantities and the vaulted basement room, too small, is due for extension; the ginger colour scheme of the lobby, the dark brown leather armchairs in steel frames, the clean-cut lines of the banisters have his stamp of approval. The rooms, some of which give onto the leafy patio, all have dark carpets, light-coloured walls and modern-design pine furniture that combine to give a sense of space and unfussiness. For example, No 54, under the roof, has a partly sloping ceiling with Velux windows, pink decor, green carpet and a fine green bathroom. The stripey curtains and bedcovers and the framed prints on the walls lift any severity. No 52, looking onto the quiet side street, is a duplex room for 2,3 or 4 where a family can enjoy a great sense of privacy. Final touch: each room has a fan for those near-tropical days that Paris can produce. If you want to jog you will be guided towards the ungated airy space of the Champ de Mars.

Rooms: 44 with bath or shower.
Price: S 480-580F; D 530-630F.
Breakfast: 40F with fruit, cereal, yoghurt and croissants "à volonté".
Meals: On request 100-150F.
Metro: Pernety; RER Denfert-Rochereau.
Bus routes: 28 58
Car park: Gaîté.

8 picture-framers still work within 100yds but nowadays Montparnasse is for modern architecture buffs with Bofill's Place de Catalogne and the sloping fountain.

Map No: 3

Hôtel Chaplain **

1bis rue Jules-Chaplain
Paris
75006

Tel: (1)43 26 47 64
Fax: (1)40 51 79 75

Management: Madame Hennessy.

The façade is a simple Paris "immeuble", neat and white on a quiet street just off the lively boulevard Montparnasse, with a few white awnings to betray the presence of an hotel. Discretion is the Chaplain's hallmark — "we don't want to alarm our clients with loud colours" — even the more colourful ground-floor public areas are softly, greenly, quietly so. Madame Hennessy and her staff are similarly quiet and unobtrusive, always ready to help and advise. The sitting and breakfast areas are united by a wall-long reproduction of Monet's bridge at Giverny (from Les Nymphéas) and water-green furniture, deep armchairs at one end, conservatory tables and chairs at the other. And the eye is led naturally out into the little courtyard where a Greek Venus and a Roman fountain-head catch the light among the greenery. This patio really makes the place. Guestrooms are on either side of the patio and onto the street, some recently redecorated, others waiting their turn. The colours are very pastel, muted, almost neutral — soft beige, textured cream, gentle stripes or florals in pink or blue. Bathrooms are small but fully 2-star equipped (including hair dryers). Showers have curtain or cabin door, the tiling is sometimes a rather smart brown pinstripe effect. Nothing earth-shaking but excellent value and the courtyard communicates peace and life at the beginning and end of the day.

Rooms: 25 with bath or shower.
Price: S 425-465F; D 470-510F; TR 675F; Q 720F.
Breakfast: 35F.
Meals: Pizza service 50-100F.
Metro: Vavin; RER Denfert Rochereau.
Bus routes: 58 68 82 92 91.
Car park: Montparnasse.

At No 11 Victor Hugo was writing "Cromwell" while at No 19 the moral philosopher Sainte-Beuve was "living in sin" with Adèle Hugo, Victor's daughter.

Map No: 4

40F

Hôtel Ferrandi

★ ★ ★

92 rue du Cherche-Midi
Paris
75006

Tel: (1)42 22 97 40
Fax: (1)45 44 89 97

Management: Madame Lafond.

Here we have a young, cheerful, efficient management team — and a drawing room that might be a picture-book study of French elegance from two centuries back (apart from the rather awful carpet) but still much sought-after in upper-class dwellings today. We particularly liked the white marble fireplace (gas/log fire in winter) and the superior club/café feel of the breakfast room with its pretend patio (in fact a wide flowerbed trellissed off from the pedestrian way beyond) that also greens the ground floor suite. If the curlicues and flounces seem heavy, you will find light relief in the many prints of Peynet's charmingly naive and intelligently suggestive drawings. This marriage of serious and witty is the soul of the place. The suite has a plush sitting room decorated with Regency-stripe paper, heavy curtains, low chairs and a superb Art Nouveau bronze-trimmed desk — then you raise your eyes to an unbelievable coloured milky glass "chandelier" with pink and green triffids growing out of it...Venetian; the bedroom is small but sports a fine Arts Deco iron bedstead in a blue and white decor leading to a pink marble bathroom leading to the lobby with its carved cupboard doors. The rest is calmer. We enjoyed the smallest bedroom with its grey hessian walls, thick-weave curtains and arched brass bedhead in an alcove of moulded wood. Now go out and observe the façade: you will see from its vast spread why all the rooms give onto the street.

Rooms: 42 with bath or shower.
Price: S/D 460-980F; ST 1280F.
Breakfast: 60F.
Meals: None
Metro: Vaneau; RER Luxembourg.
Bus routes: 39 95 48 82 68.
Car park: Hotel or Boucicaut.

Over the road is a little-known museum: Hébert, excellent draughtsman, academic painter of sensitive/sentimental portraits and landscapes. Well worth a visit.

Map No: 3

Hôtel Istria ★★

29 rue Campagne Première
Paris
75014

Tel: (1)43 20 91 82
Fax: (1)43 22 48 45

Management: Monsieur & Madame Leroux.

Despite the rather wild arty people who have lived, loved and worked here, the hall of the Istria bathes you in peace, the Kilim rugs lie quietly on the tiles before the deep leather sofas, the African carvings speak of cultures where no engines fume and the Leroux family welcome their guests with apparently genuine pleasure. Their cosmopolitan tastes do not preclude a Louis XIII reception desk or a very French carved "tallboy". They pride themselves on keeping things plain, simple and of very good quality. Thus, the contemporary bedroom furniture made of gently-curved round-edged pieces of solid elm was made for them by Jacques Athenor, the table lamps by Alain Gobert (creator of the shoggi meditation stool); much of the photography is by Man Ray (of course) and a well-known Italian client of theirs, Vasco Ascolini. One can feel that these are all friends before they are professionals. Of the two Portuguese ox-yokes decorating the vaulted breakfast room, one was their own find, the other brought back by a friend who knew they'd love it. The same discreet, simple taste prevails in the bedroom decoration where palest yellow Korean grass paper may cover the walls, pale mauve cloth stretch across the bed and mauve and gold curtains echo the two. The showers (there are 4 baths in all) are delightful quarter-circle constructions; the beds have slatted bases and firm new Dunlopillo mattresses. Charming, and thoroughly good value for a 2-star hotel near Montparnasse.

Rooms: 26 with shower or bath.
Price: S 470-520F; D 530-580F;
T 580F.
Breakfast: 40F.
Meals: None
Metro: Raspail, RER Port-Royal.
Bus routes: 91
Car park: Montparnasse.

The Istria was immortalised by Louis Aragon in a poem to his beloved Elsa; Duchamp invented his "readymade" art here; Man Ray left some photographs — enough glory?

Map No: 4

Hôtel Lenox Montparnasse   * * *

15 rue Delambre
Paris
75014

Tel: (1)43 35 34 50
Fax: (1)43 20 46 64

Management: Emmanuel Destouches.

Like the St Germain Lenox, the atmosphere here is very "in" with late-night trysters leaving the famous Rosebud bar (just two doors down and part of the artists' circuit since 1923) to seek peace in the low chairs and soft lighting of the Lenox bar (which turns into breakfast room in the morning). The list of celebrity clients is impressive indeed and some of them virtually have their own rooms here but the place is friendly, relaxed and not at all pretentious or artificial. The huge plants are triumphantly real. The evening activity certainly adds ambience but is said not to impinge on those who come to sleep. The nicest rooms (and most expensive, naturally) are the attic salon-suites with sloping ceilings, variegated original fireplaces, space and light. The furnishings are soft, contemporary and comfortable; again — we did not feel overwhelmed by "style" though each room has a fine period mirror beside the bed and a "good" piece of furniture. The owners love discovering things in junk shops, have their own suppliers of period pieces, will never disclose names and addresses... On the floor below there is an elegant high-windowed room with a balcony and a thoroughly Napoleonic theme. Bathrooms are basically, cleanly white with different-coloured friezes, and all the necessary bits. They are fairly small, as are some of the bedrooms. Bedding is firm and a stock of planks is on hand for lower back sufferers.

Rooms: 52 with bath or shower.
Price: S/D 520-640F; ST 930-960F.
Breakfast: 45F.
Meals: On request 60-50F.
Metro: Vavin, Edgar Quinet; RER Luxembourg.
Bus routes: 48 89 91 92 94 95 96
Car park: Montparnasse.

The Eurythmics band once took the hotel when recording and turned night into day, for everyone. For a month, the staff had breakfast at 7pm, made beds at midnight, and loved it!

Hôtel le Sainte-Beuve   * * *

9 rue Sainte-Beuve
Paris
75006

Tel: (1)45 48 20 07
Fax: (1)45 48 67 52

Management: Madame Compagnon.

An exceptional address on a quiet street near the Luxembourg gardens. We advise you to book early. Madame Compagnon has used all her considerable flair (and consulted David Hicks France) to renovate and redecorate an hotel that was already known and loved during the wilder days of Montparnasse. The immediate atmosphere is of light, restful (but not stuffy) luxury — quiet good taste conveyed in gentle tones and thick furnishings. In winter a log fire burns in the old marble fireplace and clients enjoy taking their drink from the deliberately modern green-trellissed, plant-covered bar to sit in a deep armchair and gaze into the flames. The attentive and efficient staff are a vital element in the sense of wellbeing you feel at the Sainte-Beuve. The hotel is small and intimate, and so are the bedrooms. The general tone is Ancient & Modern. Decorated with soft colours and contemporary "textured" materials, the pastel effect modulated by more colourful chintzes and paisleys, every room has at least one old piece of furniture — a leather-topped desk, an antique dressing-table, a polished armoire, old brass lamps — and 18th/19th-century pictures hang in rich old frames. The bathrooms are superbly modern with luxuries such as bathrobes and fine toiletries. Lastly, breakfast is a feast of croissants and brioches from the famous Mulot bakers, homemade jams from the Solitude convent and freshly-squeezed orange juice.

Rooms: 23 all with bathrooms.
Price: 700-1000F; De luxe 1050-1300F.
Breakfast: 80F.
Meals: On request 40-200F.
Metro: Notre-Dame-des-Champs, Vavin; RER Port-Royal.
Bus routes: 48 58 82 89 91 92 94 95 96
Car Park: Montparnasse.

Moral philosopher and literary critic, Sainte Beuve was known for his "bons mots" such as "The historian is a prophet of the past", "So many die before meeting themselves".

Map No: 4

Hôtel le Saint-Grégoire   ★ ★ ★
43 rue de l'Abbé Grégoire
Paris
75006

Tel: (1)45 48 23 23
Fax: (1)45 48 33 95

Management: François de Bené.

The utterly Parisian façade of the Saint-Grégoire looks even more 18th-century elegant when compared to the uglies on the other side of the street. Admire its harmonies and enjoy the peace after bustling rue de Rennes. Inside, the elegance is more contemporary with deep comfortable chairs, Indian rugs on fitted carpets and a colour scheme (matching ashtrays) designed by David Hicks France — plum, old pink and ginger materials, a red doormat, a brass-ringed half-curtain for privacy, a simple classical fireplace (fires in winter), very modern unprecious dried flower arrangements by Jules des Prés and a real welcome. We found the atmosphere delicious. Sit in the little reading room beside the green mini-patio, listen to gentle classical music, admire the antiques lovingly collected by owner Lucie Agaud. In one terrace bedroom, you will find a set of intriguing folding coathooks, in the other, a most unusual thickset writing desk that bears witness to a life of solid serious work. Room sizes vary but every one has a genuinely old piece or two and the mirror frames are lovely. Pinks and browns are favoured, including bathroom marble, bedcovers are mostly bright white piqué, curtains light florals and the private-home feel is helped by the rugs strewn everywhere. The rooms over the street are larger than the others, some with two windows, though of course it is delightful to have breakfast on the terrace of one of those special rooms.

Rooms: 20 (2 with terrace), one suite, all with bathrooms (1 shower).
Price: ST & T with terrace: 1390F; D (shower) with terrace: 930F; others 790-930F.
Breakfast: 60F with fresh orange juice.
Meals: The owners also run nearby restaurant La Marlotte.
Metro: St Placide, RER Luxembourg.
Bus routes: 63 68 84 89 92 94
Car park: Opposite hotel.

Abbé Grégoire was a Revolutionary bishop who proposed ending the feudal Right of Primogeniture (eldest boy takes all) and got France to abolish slavery in 1794.

     Map No: 4

Champ de Mars & Eiffel Tower

•

Ecole Militaire

•

Invalides & Esplanade

•

Bridges over the Seine

Invalides – Eiffel Tower

Débattre
Debate

Se débattre
Struggle

Hôtel Saint-Dominique **
62 rue Saint-Dominique
Paris
75007

Tel: (1)47 05 51 44
Fax: (1)47 05 81 28

Management: Madame Petit & Monsieur Tible.

Antoine Tible is the life and soul of the place. He is enthusiastic, energetic and communicates vastly. No wonder some Great Names one would expect to find in ritzier places come again and again for the discreet address and "old friends" atmosphere — you too will enjoy the welcome, be treated to huge amounts of attention and conversation and just love his English. There is a rustic feel about the lobby — maybe a reminder of the convent this was when the area was far from the city, rural and traffic-free? Now go through into the courtyard and feel how the walls exude that peace still. It is a deliciously disorganised riot of creepers, pots, sheds and parasols — a lovely spot for breakfast on warm mornings and rooms that give onto it will hear birdsong. The courtyard leads to the second building which only has two floors (no lift). The rooms here, off a country-house-style blue and brown velvet staircase, are decorated with country prints, furnished with pine or brass beds and small bits of furniture (not much storage space). Downstairs you can reach the single-storey third building at the back. It is secluded all right but some rooms look straight into the rooms across the alley. The main building has some larger and very attractive "executive" rooms. The overall impression is of an old much-loved family house adapted over the generations, whence the split levels, bits of passageway, curious angles and nooks. Wonderful!

Rooms: 34 with bath or shower.
Price: S 430F; D 475-515F;
TR 610-705.
Breakfast: 40F.
Meals: None.
Metro: Latour-Maubourg, Invalides
(+RER+Air France bus).
Bus routes: 69 63 49 28.
Car park: Invalides.

200 years ago, the "Gros Caillou" stream flowed here where poor but inexpensive washerwomen were known to ruin your linen. The rich sent theirs to be washed in Holland.

70F

exc JCB

Hôtel le Tourville

★ ★ ★ ★

16 avenue de Tourville
Paris
75007

Tel: (1)47 05 62 62
Fax: (1)47 05 43 90

Management: Véronique Maas.

On a calm tree-lined avenue, the Tourville is a comfortable, reasonably-priced 4-star hotel — but the welcome you receive is worth a skyful of stars. I do prefer talking to someone behind an antique desk with fresh flowers to tackling someone hidden by a high counter! The soft, cushioned impression in the sitting area is due to deep carpets with Turkish and Indian rugs (they lighten and colour the whole hotel), plush sofas, indoor shutters to filter the afternoon sun and muted Vivaldi. Sensuous colours and shapes abound — butter yellow, fir green, gatepost ornaments on an Empire console, a miniature Venus of Milo in the tiny planted patio. Inside is out and outside in. I loved the ironical decorative touches, full of intelligence and fun. Each room has two or three "finds" — a brass-handled chest of drawers, a Regency writing table, a gilt-framed mirror. And more irony in the parody paintings. The ground-floor triple room is large with its own terrace, a jacuzzi bath and a fascinating neo-classical group of nude women. The junior suites are also generous with space and light — and more kitschy girls in frames. I felt some rooms were small for the category but they have good storage space and super modern bathrooms (thick fluffy towels, marble), possibly with a Victorian clothes horse or an old nursery chair in contrast. To offset such simple sophistication the vaulted breakfast room has a rustic air with coconut matting, cane chairs and a rough patina on the pale peach-washed walls.

Rooms: 28 (4 with private terrace) & 2 junior suites with jacuzzi.
Price: S 690-890F; D 690-990F; with terrace 1390F; ST 1490-1690F.
Breakfast: 60F.
Meals: On request 45-400F.
Metro: Ecole Militaire; RER Invalides.
Bus routes: 29 48 80 82 87 92
Car park: Ecole Militaire.

Tourville was a romantic admiral called Anne (sic) who fought pirates in the Mediterranean and spent the 1690s locked in naval battles with the English in the Channel.

Map No: 3

40F

exc Diners

Hôtel de la Tulipe ★ ★

33 rue Malar
Paris
75007

Tel: (1)45 51 67 21
Fax: (1)47 53 96 37

Management: Monsieur & Madame Fortuit.

What a delightful place! What a lovely family! We found the lobby full of happy life and the scent of a huge bunch of syringa brought from their country weekend. A small intimate hotel, it was once a convent and has only one upper floor with rooms set around the wildly green, honeysuckled, cobbled courtyard or over the quiet street; some have windows on to both. They seem small but they all represent at least two cells...and two are in the former chapel. It has been a hotel since the influx of visitors to the Exposition Universelle in 1900. There are beams and exposed stones, Japanese grass paper, simple pine or cane furniture (though the peacock-tail bedhead and chair don't qualify as simple), patchwork bedcovers and white curtains, or bright Provençal curtains and cream covers. Many of the bath/shower-rooms have blue-pattern country-style tiling (quite appropriate here) and all are perfectly adequate. The one room without a wc has its own across the landing. The breakfast room is beside the reception; or sit in the courtyard with the birds. The croissants come fresh each day from the local bakery, not from an industrial chain. A tearoom/salad bar will be installed by autumn 1995 so light lunches will also be available — and quite delicious I am sure they will be. Above all, with the unpretentiousness of the Fortuit family and their hotel we remember their smiles and relaxed manner and so, most certainly, will you.

Rooms: 20 with shower or bath.
Price: S 428-498F; D 498-548F.
Breakfast: 40F with cheese and baker's croissants.
Meals: Light lunches and snacks.
Metro & RER: Invalides, Pont de l'Alma.
Bus routes: 49 63 69 80 92
Car park: Rue Malar.

"Before the war, rue Malar was full of little shops — a button-mender (for tiny cloth-covered buttons), a seller of wine by the glass, all killed by the supermarkets." A former tenant, 55 years on.

Map No: 1

Hôtel Wallace ★★★

89 rue Fondary
Paris
75015

Tel: (1)45 78 83 30
Fax: (1)40 58 19 43

Management: Dalynda Betina.

The Wallace may seem a little off-centre but we like it for its space and airiness and quiet (although some of the benefit may be lost with the radio playing in the lobby?) and attention to guests' needs. The courtyard-garden has been glazed in and become more a conservatory — perfect in cool weather, possibly a bit stuffy on hot summer evenings despite the many openings. But the former garden is still here in the old cobbles, the fountain head, the statues and the ivy. The sitting area is large, palely floral and temptingly cushioned, especially as you will be provided with the right newspaper (Russian if you are Russian, for example) if you stay a while. The hotel consists of two low buildings round the courtyard. Some rooms are reached along outside galleries: it has the feel of a seaside boarding house or a Swiss chalet. And the decor may have something Swiss about it too — plain and modern, with cloth-covered walls, colourful bedcovers and curtains, adequate bathrooms and always the peace. The Wallace in question was Sir Richard of the fine art collection who inherited the Bagatelle estate on the edge of Paris and, legend has it, came to view his possessions, found he couldn't get a glass of drinking water for love or money and donated 100 drinking fountains to the people of Paris where they could always be sure of healthy water running free. They are all over the city, green painted and supported by four lovely ladies forever fair.

Rooms: 35 with bath or shower.
Price: S 550F; D 650F.
Breakfast: 50F, huge.
Meals: From caterer 50-200F.
Metro: La Motte-Picquet-Grenelle, Emile Zola; RER Javel.
Bus routes: 49 80.
Car park: Hotel.

Map No: 3

In 1823, Fondary was one of the spec developers of this far-flung wasteland behind the Ecole Militaire, previously used mainly for military executions.

Chaillot Museums & Gardens

•

Museum of Modern Art

•

Guimet Museum

•

Radio France building

Trocadéro – Passy

Jouer son va-tout
Stake one's all

Etre passible de...
Be liable to... (sentence, fine, etc.)

Hôtel Frémiet ★ ★ ★
6 avenue Frémiet
Paris
75016

Tel: (1)45 24 52 06
Fax: (1)42 88 77 46

Management: Monsieur Fourmond.

The steep little street is a glorious symmetrical piece of architecture built by Albert Veque in 1913, all in curves and juttings, stone carvings and corbels, garlands and figleaf fantasies. They were built as superior apartment blocks and the Frémiet has brilliantly kept the volumes and decorations of its beginnings. The owner is proud to declare that guestrooms are NOT rational here but guests are most carefully attended to. From the lovely staircase (red carpeting with brass rods and superb original leaded and painted windows), each landing has a grand double doorway into the 10-foot-ceilinged 160sq.m. apartment, now split up of course. The former drawing room, now a good-sized bedroom, has a fine curved window onto a balcony with view of the Seine, original mouldings and panelling; the master bedroom has become another excellent guestroom. The former kitchen is a huge bathroom with sensual matt-white double basins and a cockerel crowing in the tiling. Overall, it is a lesson in French apartment design just before society collapsed into the Great War. The degree of comfort quite matches the grand atmosphere. Classic Louis XV and Louis XVI pieces alongside some built-in practicalities so that all rooms have space. Rooms that have been recently redone have "modern" colour schemes (blue walls and chairs with white paintwork plus a blue and white bathroom, for example); others are more traditional pastels; all are fully soundproofed. And the welcome is high-class too.

Rooms: 36 with shower or bath (inc disabled).
Price: S 500-720F; D 650-915F; ST 1300F.
Breakfast: 40F
Meals: From caterer 100-200F.
Metro: Passy; RER Champ de Mars.
Bus routes: 72 32.
Car park: Rue Frémiet.

The nearby rue des Eaux was where the female-fertility waters sprang in 1650...and dried up in the 1780s. So the Wine Museum was built there instead.

Map No: 3

Hôtel Massenet   ***

5 bis rue Massenet
Paris
75116

Tel: (1)45 24 43 03
Fax: (1)45 24 41 39

Management: Monsieur Mathieu.

Since 1927, three generations of Mathieu have cultivated the arts of welcome and attentiveness to others at the Massenet behind its superb multi-balconied and encorbelled 1900s façade. The human reception is as rich and rounded as the wood panelling and arched glazing of the lobby. The main staff have been here for 15 years and really know their clients, whence a comfortable club atmosphere round the bar. This gives onto the little patio garden where breakfast can be taken amongst the flower pots on fine mornings. Or you can delight in the original carved panelling and moulded ceiling of the breakfast room, a haven just off the fashionable shopping street of Passy. Upstairs, the bedrooms are fairly ordinary and thoroughly comfortable with beige-based muted tones and nothing invasive. There are bits of antique furniture, plenty of cupboard space and lots of light. The top floor offers two rooms with terraces for intimate breakfasts in the sun or evening drinks overlooking the (tip of the) Eiffel Tower (the ugly concrete trellises are due to be removed). Rooms are being renovated, floor by floor. We definitely preferred the new clear, gentle decor here with concealed lighting and fine print curtains; the owners are happy with the work in progress too. They have cleverly kept one of the original 1930s bathrooms with rounded-edge mosaics ("you don't find that any more") and the fabulous Art Nouveau staircase windows ("collectors' pieces").

Rooms: 41 with bath or shower.
Price: S 485F; D 660-760F.
Breakfast: 40F.
Meals: On request 50-200F.
Metro: La Muette, Passy; RER Muette-Boulainvilliers.
Bus routes: 22 32 52
Car park: Franck & Fils.

300 years ago, society ladies trekked out to the sticks to take the waters. Passy still attracts fashionable Parisiennes — who live, shop and give coffee parties here.

Arc de Triomphe
•
Haute couture
•
Grand Palais – Petit Palais
•
Place de la Concorde
•
La Madeleine church

Etoile – Champs Elysées

Ils ne savent où donner de la tête
They don't know which way to turn

Induire quelqu'un en erreur
Lead someone astray

exc Diners

Hôtel des Champs-Elysées **

2 rue d'Artois
Paris
75008

Tel: (1)43 59 11 42
Fax: (1)45 61 00 61

Management: Madame Monteil.

Nothing is too much for Madame Monteil. She will even provide a little talc to ease swollen feet into tight boots during a heatwave. The art of hospitality has been handed down from her grandparents, first in the family to own the hotel; their prewar pictures adorn one wall. The unpretentious façade on a quiet street speaks for the simple, gracious reception you will receive inside. There are deep leather sofas in the lobby and light conservatory chairs near the bar beneath a bright perspective of obelisk and triumphal arch. There is elegance in the staircase (especially the 4th-floor addition) with its blue and grey decor. Bedrooms are fully soundproofed; each is fitted with a made-to-measure stained-wood bedhead and framed desktop unit incorporating the minibar and giving a neat finish. Covers and curtains are often made of English material, subtly coordinated with pastel-pink, cream-sponged or turquoise walls for lighter or darker effect; the wall-mounted bedside lights are cleancut and well-placed and the mirrored cupboards provide adequate storage. Bathrooms are small but just as recently renovated in smart grey, silver, black and white tiles or beige marble and the fittings (including some ingenious quarter-round shower stalls) are in keeping. With baker's croissants and bread for breakfast (nothing industrial here), we thought we had found remarkable value in an expensive neighbourhood — and exceptional human contact.

Rooms: 31 with shower; 4 with bath.
Price: D (shower) 470F; T (bath) 540F.
Breakfast: 39F.
Meals: None.
Metro: St Philippe du Roule, Franklin Roosevelt; RER Charles de Gaulle-Etoile.
Bus routes: 32 73
Car park: Rue La Boétie.

Amazingly, in the present-day artificiality of the area, this street was the Royal (and Revolutionary, and Imperial) plant nursery from 1640 to 1826.

Map No: 1

Hôtel Centre Ville Matignon ★★★

3 rue de Ponthieu
Paris
75008

Tel: (1)42 25 73 01
Fax: (1)42 56 01 39

Management: Alain Michaud.

Paris has plenty of imitations of the 1920s Modern Style. The Matignon is no copy, it is genuine, real, authentic 1924 and we love it. Enter the rectangle-upon-rectangle glazed porch, walk along the 3-coloured mosaic floor, stand under the perfect curves of the ceiling light that grows out of all those straight lines: your skin understands what they were saying. The lift is 1924 too — all iron frame and engraved glass panels, a collector's dream. You will be welcomed by people who are relaxed yet sensitive to your needs, a delightful contrast to the smart head-office atmosphere and laissez-aller of the Champs Elysées. The geometric style continues up the stairs. Each panelled door opens to reveal a large original fresco (landscapes or near-abstract still lifes, they are very proper given the purpose for which these rooms were designed). Bathrooms have Arts Deco mod cons (basins on heavy stands with antique taps, old-fashioned tiling and trim), though some bits are showing their age. Otherwise, the bedrooms are discreet with dark carpets, heavy curtains, coordinated quilted or textured bedcovers and head cushions (a bow to 1990s fashion), black metal bedside lights (another), fine inner blinds and adequate storage space. Rooms are far from enormous but they all have a lobby (except the junior suites where a larger lobby houses the third bed and the cupboard). The Amadeus Bar is your breakfast room — and an evening venue for the Parisian "in" crowd.

Rooms: 23 inc 4 junior suites.
Price: S 590-900F; D 690-1000F;
ST 850-1500F.
Breakfast: 55F with fresh orange juice
& cheeses.
Meals: Restaurant "Chez Moi" menus
110-150F. Deliveries 70-130F.
Metro: Champs Elysées-Clémenceau;
RER Charles de Gaulle-Etoile.
Bus routes: 28 32 42 49 73 93
Car park: Champs Elysées.

Mansions were built here in the 1700s (the Elysée for La Pompadour); the "Elysian Fields" were covered with modest houses in the 1800s; in the 1920s, activity was less modest...

Map No: 1

Hôtel de l'Elysée ★ ★ ★

2 rue des Saussaies
Paris
75008

Tel: (1)42 65 29 25
Fax: (1)42 65 64 28

Management: Madame Lafond.

This is not a wildly exciting hotel; it is just good solid value. And for those with a thing about security, many rooms overlook the Ministry of the Interior with its grand entrance on the Place Beauveau! Like its left-bank sister the Ferrandi, the Elysée has fake marble panels hand-painted on the staircase walls (an art of bygone days), a real white marble fireplace and many canopied beds. Its theme is "Restauration" which, in France, refers to the early 19th-century post-Napoleonic (and short-lived) restoration of the monarchy. The basic intention is to make you feel comfortable in a chintzy country-house way with a few dramatically baroque details — a study of lamps and light fittings reveals some astounding gilded harvest sprays and spiky vegetables that might have grown in a pterodactyl's field. Otherwise, quilting, padding and subdued velvets are the order of the day. As usual, some "standard" rooms are really quite small, but there will be a moulded ceiling or a hand-painted cupboard. Some are fairly sombre in shades of green, brown and beige, others are covered in bright flowers. The deluxe rooms on the corner are nice with their three windows and generous space. The top-floor rooms have most character — sloping ceilings, visible timbers and funny-shaped spaces. It is all plush and peaceful, there's a real bar to perch at for your aperitif and marble-topped tables for breakfast. A comfort to come back to.

Rooms: 32 + 2 suites with bath or shower.
Price: D 600-980F; T 700-840F; ST 1320F.
Breakfast: 60F.
Meals: None.
Metro: Champs Elysées, Miromesnil; RER Opéra-Auber.
Bus routes: 52
Car park: Hôtel Bristol.

The "tenant" of the Place Beauveau is the chief of police; "saussaie" comes from "saule" = birch. In the days of birching, did the police grow their own?

Map No: 1

 exc Diners

Hôtel Résidence Lord Byron ★★★

5 rue de Chateaubriand
Paris
75008

Tel: (1)43 59 89 98
Fax: (1)42 89 46 04

Management: Madame Daurer.

Although it is just a short step from the glitzy lights and fast-food spots of the Champs Elysées (who would want to be a blessed soul in THIS afterlife?), we liked the Lord Byron for the luxury of its garden-courtyard, even if it is basically a traditional business area hotel. Half its rooms give onto this quite generous square of birches, bamboo, shrubbery and flowerbeds. Birds, not honking motor cars, will herald your waking and you can have a summer breakfast among the blooms (and on the plastic furniture...). Otherwise, the style is set by the lobby where draperies, flounces and swags adorn the panels and arches and little French tables and plush chairs reflect prettily in large mirrors. Up a few stairs to the reception desk and sitting/breakfast room which is again richly damasked, thickly carpeted and softly welcoming. The staff are also welcoming, be they at reception or in service — nothing obtrusive or unexpected, just careful attention. No two rooms are the same. The suites are obviously the largest, their two areas (sitting, with convertible sofa, and sleeping) separated by heavy curtains. Colour schemes can be bold — blue carpet, red chairs, chintz bedcovers — there are antique chests, fireside chairs and low tables. The bathrooms are fully equipped and mostly beige. The ground-floor garden rooms are smaller and darker but so quiet...and yellow or bright blue walls lighten the effect. Some beds may be a little soft but this is still a haven in a wild world.

Rooms: 31 with bath or shower.
Price: S 650-800F; D 800-900F;
ST 1250F.
Breakfast: 50F
Meals: None.
Metro: George V; RER Charles de
Gaulle-Etoile.
Bus routes: 73
Car park: 5 rue de Berri.

For the French, Byron is a Great Romantic Figure, although he had no connection with France. But rejecting all things English, was he not an honorary Frenchman?

Map No: 1

 exc Diners

Hôtel Mayflower ★ ★ ★

3 rue Chateaubriand
Paris
75008

Tel: (1)45 62 57 46
Fax: (1)42 56 32 38

Management: Madame Benoît.

It may sound strange, but the Mayflower is Lord Byron's sister, next door and under the same management. It is just as reliably comfortable, traditional in style, gentle in reception, only it does not have the advantage of a secluded garden. But with a bit of sibling understanding... What it does have is a really rather delightful basement breakfast room (air conditioned) all decked out to look like a ship's saloon, right down to the vasty seas "seen" through the mirror "windows". At street level, the large bar and sitting room are completely French in their display of panelled walls, marble fireplace, deep-sprung or upright velvet armchairs and tasteful ornaments. The flowers are part real part silk. The staircase and landings, lined with simple Japanese grass paper, have some interesting curves to show; admire the model of a ship that is not the Mayflower at the bottom. The bedrooms are decorated in the same good if rather neutral taste. The walls are refreshingly white or off-white. Many rooms (except on the top floor) have the same functionally-designed fitted desk top covering a 3-drawer unit and the minibar, and decent cupboard space. Materials are chintzy prints and velvet upholstery, carpets are rich dark colours, beds are cane or painted wood. And like its neighbour, it is all softness and quiet.

Rooms: 24 with bath or shower.
Price: S 650-800F; D 800-950F; extra bed 120F.
Breakfast: 50F.
Meals: None.
Metro: George V; RER Charles de Gaulle-Etoile.
Bus routes: 73
Car park: 5 rue de Berri.

At No 2 rue Washington lives a near-extinct species: a shirt tailor who will take your measurements, make your pattern, offer a superb choice of cloth and mail the finished articles.

Map No: 1

Hôtel Majestic   ★ ★ ★ ★
29 rue Dumont d'Urville
Paris
75116

Tel: (1)45 00 83 70
Fax: (1)45 00 29 48

Management: Madame Baverez.

Yes, this uninspiring 1960s building really is your 4-star hotel, in a double time warp, somehow. Once inside the pinched doorway, you will gasp at so much pre-war generosity of space and outpouring of (very sober) French style. Period furniture (some fine pieces, many good copies), tapestries, Persian carpets, panelling, botanical and ornithological prints soon make you forget the breeze blocks of the construction. The sitting and breakfast areas are so French you feel you might convert by osmosis. The youthful staff, however, have that elegant intelligent friendliness that can be one of the saving graces of Parisian hotels; they remove any apprehension the formality might arouse. Rooms are also vast but you could be at home: each door has its own brass letterbox and doorbell! Some even have kitchens, now used for luggage storage, and the smallest rooms have space for a few dance steps. Some bathrooms have a 1960s feel — for example, vivid yellow square tiles "brightened" by a lime green frieze and real character in the old-fashioned but beautifully-kept fittings. The Penthouse at the very top has a good-size terrace with magnificent views across Paris as well as a large Regency-style bedroom and drawing-room. Storage space is endless and the wall-mounted light fittings are an appropriately amazing design in gilt bronze and matt blue china. This place is utterly quiet and you can sink into an other-worldly cocoon — spoil yourself and enjoy it!

Rooms: 30 with bathrooms.
Price: S 920-1170F; D 1170-1470F; ST 1820F; Penthouse 1920F.
Breakfast: 60F.
Meals: Delivered from Hotel Raphael restaurant 60-200F.
Metro: Kléber; RER Charles de Gaulle-Etoile.
Bus routes: 22 30 31 52 73 92
Car park: Rue Lauriston.

Wherefore Majestic? From 1904-1934, the family owned The Majestic — 600 superb rooms of international renown on avenue Kléber. Here we have the baby grandchild.

Map No: 1

Parc Monceau gardens
•
St Ferdinand
•
Bois de Boulogne
•
Jardin d'Acclimatation

Etoile – Porte Maillot

 30F

 exc Diners

Hôtel de Banville ★ ★ ★
166 boulevard Berthier
Paris
75017

Tel: (1)42 67 70 16
Fax: (1)44 40 42 77

Management: Mademoiselle Marianne Lambert.

Walk into the Banville and you walk into an upper-class Parisian apartment. Recognize the sensuous curves of the Arts Deco wrought-iron stair rail, the wholly French period furniture, the upright armchairs, the soft elegance of inherited style — nothing here is mass-produced. In keeping with the decor, you will be genuinely welcomed into the warm Lambert family who have run the hotel for three generations with a loyal band of "old retainers" (for the last 30 years, Jean-Pierre Bukovinski has lovingly renovated the furniture and painted the pictures that grace your room; he knows every nook and loves the place like his own home). They all speak English. They all love working here. The motto of the house might be "Meet the client's expectation before it is put into words". Rooms are constantly being redesigned and redecorated with much loving care and talent by the two Lambert ladies. They use careful colour-coding, they know how to mix modern and period furniture, their rooms are full of light, pale colours and intimacy. Theirs is a gentle, airy, soft-quilt-on-firm-mattress touch and their bathrooms are utterly modern. The building is set back from the boulevard, some rooms look out over its leafy plane trees, others over quiet courtyards; from the very top, 8th-floor room you can see — mais oui — la Tour Eiffel. Excellent public transport to all parts of Paris.

Rooms: 39 (5 with "twinnable" king-size beds) with bathrooms.
Price: S 635F; D 760F; TR 860F.
Breakfast: 45F, 70F or 80F + à la carte.
Meals: Light meals 30F to 150F.
Metro: Porte de Champerret, Pereire (& RER).
Bus routes: 92 84 93 PC
Car park: Rue de Courcelles.

Covered with titles and glory by Napoleon, Berthier died defenestrated, either due to a fit of insanity or the actions of 6 masked men "seen in the vicinity at that time". We shall never know.

Map No: 1

Hôtel Centre Ville Etoile ***
6 rue des Acacias
Paris
75017

Tel: (1)43 80 56 18
Fax: (1)47 54 93 43

Management: Alain Michaud.

This tiny hotel has a very definite style; for once, tiny has not meant cosy. We liked it for its difference. The shiny black reception desk — and the 20-foot ficus tree — are in a 3-storey galleried well of light that gives onto a quiet, plant-filled cul-de-sac. We were very taken with the ingenuity and originality of the space. The view from the top gallery is an engineer's delight, all metal frame and curtain wall. The decor may be a little sombre for some, based on an Arts Deco style that dictates the black and white colour scheme, with a chromatic glance at American Surrealism in the shape of a large original oil by a 1930s artist. There are prints from American cartoon strips and black carpeting with slippy grey-white stripes like running water everywhere. The rooms are small but spaces are rationally used, though storage remains limited. They can be masculine (pale brown wall covering, brown and black abstract bedheads, covers and curtains, one black and one... red chair), or more pastel-shaded (blue covers with 1950s-style coloured-print curtains), or elegant white, cream and grey mixtures. Bathrooms have white fittings, gentle round basins, restful grey tiling, lots of mirrors. In contrast, bright red oriental-print table cloths (on black tables...) and airy Bauhaus wire chairs enliven the basement breakfast room. With so few rooms, staff have plenty of time to be friendly, helpful and really welcoming.

Rooms: 15 with bathrooms.
Price: S 590-800F; D 690-900F;
T 750-950F.
Breakfast: 55F.
Meals: On request 100F upwards.
Metro: Argentine; RER & Air France bus: Charles de Gaulle-Etoile.
Bus routes: 73
Car park: 24 rue des Acacias.

In 1834, Louis Philippe's heir apparent took a fast bend nearby, fell out of his carriage and was killed. Banal? Yes, but few crash victims have Byzantine chapels built in their memory (place St Ferdinand).

Map No: 1

exc JCB

Hôtel Cheverny   ★ ★ ★

7 villa Berthier
Paris
75017

Tel: (1)43 80 46 42
Fax: (1)47 63 26 62

Management: Monsieur Brillant & Monsieur Gillot.

The Cheverny has the character conveyed by unexpected spaces, vistas and twists in its layout, every one of them used to horticultural effect. The owners' gardening talk was great fun! With two buildings and various gaps in between, they have created a series of miniature hanging gardens, terraces and patios overlooked by glass passages and landings transformed into tempting little sitting areas. There are plants everywhere and flowers of all colours in summer. So just a stone's throw from the lively boulevard (and 5 minutes walk from the Porte Maillot conference centre, 15 from the Arc de Triomphe), here is a place to sleep in peaceful and stylish surroundings. The style is cleanly modern with a taste of the 1930s in the bucket chairs. Colour schemes are pale and restful, dove-grey with dark blue, deep biscuit with pale cream and "ethnic" woven patchwork materials for a touch of fresh brightness. The tailor-made bedroom units are elegant and unobtrusive with disguised minibars, mirror-fronted cupboards, suitcase spaces underneath (a minor but clever detail) and firm beds. Bathrooms are just as coolly attractive with a neat clothes-line (another good mark). Rooms ending in 10 have two windows, one double and one single sofabed and a separate wc. Other rooms are smaller — as reflected in the price. In summer, you can breakfast in the trellissed and leafy patio, otherwise in the well-ventilated vaulted cellar.

Rooms: 48 with bath or shower.
Price: S 510F; D 570F; TR 650-820F.
Breakfast: 40F.
Meals: None.
Metro: Porte Champerret; RER Pereire.
Bus routes: 84 92 93 PC
Car park: Porte Champerret.

In 1874, in the heyday of steam, the Boulevard Berthier was chosen to test a new single-rail steam-tram. Not a huge success, it was not put into production.

Hôtel Eber   ✳ ✳ ✳

18 rue Léon Jost
Paris
75017

Tel: (1)46 22 60 70
Fax: (1)47 63 01 01

Management: Jean-Marc Eber.

Jean-Marc Eber will quickly communicate his enthusiasm, his pleasure in personal contact with guests to his small charming hotel. We liked the lighthearted approach married to very professional management. (The Eber is a "Relais du Silence".) Here you may meet top models, fashion designers or other film folk appropriate to this smart neighbourhood. The many photographs and documents that decorate the walls will lead you through the building of the Statue of Liberty, two streets away. And you can borrow a house umbrella in your hour of need — a very superior touch, perhaps inspired by the two umbrella-toting slave boys sitting on the mantelpiece or by the owner's years in the 4-star world? The intimate salon and bar/breakfast area are simply nice places to sit and there is a little green patio for al fresco breakfast (served at any hour with 15 sorts of jam and 3 teas). The rooms vary in size, some are quite small but with all mod cons, some have grandly high ceilings; the apartments are large enough for families. The duplex with private terrace is particularly seductive. The colours are fairly neutral, unobtrusive beiges with pastel print draperies and storage space is mostly adequate. Bathrooms are also nicely tiled and fitted. We liked the "olde" look of the cast-iron towel rails on wooden brackets. A delightful yet professional host who wants each guest to be so at home here that he/she comes back.

Rooms: 18 with bath or shower.
Price: S/D 610-660F;
ST 1050-1360F.
Breakfast: 50F.
Meals: On request 50-250F.
Metro: Courcelles; RER Charles de Gaulle-Etoile.
Bus routes: 84
Car park: 200m Elf.

Walk in the nearby Parc Monceau, one of Paris's finest, and consider your luck: it was originally (1770s) private, the Duke of Chartres' country cottage garden.

Map No: 1

Hôtel Etoile-Maillot   ★★★
10 rue du Bois de Boulogne
Paris
75116

Tel: (1)45 00 42 60
Fax: (1)45 00 55 89

Management: Madame Vidalenc.

The Etoile-Maillot is Edith Vidalenc's first hotel and is totally different from the Pergolèse : it is as traditional as the Pergolèse is contemporary. It is small — there is no breakfast room — and friendly, one might almost say intimate. An old and very French chest of drawers (Louis XV curves and counter-curves, twisty bronze fittings, marble top) surmounted by a landscape in oils in a suitably ornate gilt frame give the lobby the feel of a private sitting room and the receptionist will welcome you as a guest rather than a client. Upstairs, the rooms echo this old French style. Each room has carefully chosen period furniture, there are lots of leather-covered studded "fireside" chairs and little marble-topped tables. The beds are large and the colours are comfortable; redecoration is continuous. No 27 has biscuit walls and moss green draperies for an autumnal atmosphere; No 26 is very masculine in ginger and beige. Materials are from the Pierre Frey collection, wall-coverings are in soft peachskin cloth or fashionable sponged wash. Some light fittings in curly bronze or opalescent flowers match the old furniture; the bathrooms are finished in marble. On the corner of two side streets away from the throngs of the main thoroughfare, it is quiet with a touch of class, friendly and unpretentious.

Rooms: 28 with bath or shower.
Price: S 580-710F; D 630-760F;
ST 890F.
Breakfast: 40F included.
Meals: None.
Metro: Argentine; RER + Air France
bus Porte Maillot.
Bus routes: 73
Car park: Avenue Foch.

The little streets of this diminutive "village" so close to the great Elysian Fields are home to greengrocers, haberdashers, hairdressers... and at least 4 antique dealers.

Map No: 1

Hôtel de Neuville ✱ ✱ ✱
3 rue Verniquet
Paris
75017

Tel: (1)43 80 26 30
Fax: (1)43 80 38 55

Management: Madame Beherec.

Its white stone façade with geranium-filled windowboxes overlooks a quiet square just off the boulevard Pereire. The large airy split-level lobby, full of light from the arched windows, feels like a club with oak-toned armchairs, low tables, bar stools and interesting works by a contemporary painter (the artist changes every few months). Your eye is then drawn past two pairs of Ionic columns towards the little patio, all greenery and pots and lovely stones giving a sense of space and peace. And the "basement" breakfast room has a wonderful surprise: the patio is down here too, the green light and air skilfully augmented with mirrors. This is definitely a family-run hotel. Madame manages it with Monsieur (they also own the left-bank Clos Médicis), does the cooking, designs and makes the draperies, supervises her children's drawing sessions when they are out of school and is still a charming, relaxed hostess. There are two honeymoon guestrooms sporting canopied beds with voluptuous blowsy curtains. The rooms over the boulevard are a good size, well-lit and the higher you are the more you can see of the Sacré Coeur. Colours are soft orange with salmon pink in bold chintzes or more gentle florals; the furniture is comfortable with some brass bedsteads, some plain pine; there is decent storage space, old lamps and Old Masters to remind us of the building's 19th-century origins. A quiet, friendly place to stay.

Rooms: 28 with bathrooms.
Price: S 706Fr, D 712F.
Breakfast: 55F with cheese, yoghurt, hard-boiled eggs, fresh fruit, cereals.
Meals: Light lunches 100-120F on weekdays.
Metro & RER: Pereire.
Bus routes: 84 92 93
Car park: Hotel.

The environment was improved 3 years ago when a nursery school and tennis courts were built over the metro. Add the trees and you have the complete village atmosphere.

Map No: 1

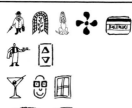

Hôtel Pergolèse

★ ★ ★ ★

3 rue Pergolèse
Paris
75116

Tel: (1)40 67 96 77
Fax: (1)45 00 12 11

Management: Madame Vidalenc.

This hotel is a refreshing festival of work by contemporary designers. From room shapes, use of light and materials to small tables, glassware and toiletries — every detail counts. Edith Vidalenc joined forces with Rena Dumas (whose family owns Hermès) and Philippe Starck to produce a sleek but warmly colourful, curvaceously human hotel. Hilton McConnico did the pictures. Materials are wood and leather, glass bricks and polished metal. She also takes great care over staff attitudes : the small faithful team at reception know all the regular clients and are leagues away from the frosty 4-star feel that so often passes for deluxe. The leitmotiv shape is the arch over the main doorway, repeated in leaf-like ash bedheads, lobby sofas before curved glass walls onto the patio, Starck's table legs and Andrée Putman's chrome "tureen" washbasins. The general tone is mutedly smart so the multi-coloured breakfast room suddenly reminds you of a primary school — great fun. Indeed, not taking oneself too seriously while doing a really professional job is the keynote here. Rooms, fairly small except for the top-floor Pergolèse room, are all similarly furnished in pale wood, leather, a specially-designed disguise for minibar and television, thick unpatterned curtains and white bedcovers in a super-soft leather-like material. The star Pergolèse room, lit by sloping rooflights, is a small masterpiece, if you don't mind having your (superb) bathroom partly in the bedroom (separate wc).

Rooms: 40 with bath or shower.
Price: S 1220F; D 1320F; Pergolèse 1520F; 3 small rooms 860-960F.
Breakfast: 75F good value.
Meals: Very light meals 50-200F.
Metro: Argentine; RER + Air France bus Porte Maillot.
Bus routes: 73
Car park: Place Saint Ferdinand.

The Porte Maillot's expanding conference centre and roaring traffic were not ever thus: from 1830 to 1930 it was a huge, much-frequented fun fair, the "Luna Park".

Map No: 1

Hôtel Regent's Garden   ★ ★ ★
6 rue Pierre Demours
Paris
75017

Tel: (1)45 74 07 30
Fax: (1)40 55 01 42

Management: Mademoiselle Le Guellaut & Monsieur Frot.

The Regent's Garden was built in the 1850s by Napoleon III for his personal doctor and looks "as new". It is heavy, opppressive ....and perfectly amazing. As you come across the leafy courtyard (cum carpark) and up the grand staircase, watch for the chandelier: a period piece in silver bronze with clear and mauve glass danglers that cascade down to a great solid ball of crystal. Dazzling. Plus mouldings and columns, ruches and swags, tassels and fringes, featherweight gilded coffee tables and solid button chairs in a dominant red-and-yellow pallette. We wallowed until, starved for a piece of plain wood, we looked further and, merciful heaven, saw the garden, a riot of shrubberies, flowerbeds, creepers and acacias. You can sit in this miraculous piece of nature and enjoy the contrast. Authenticity is the aim in guestrooms too. All different, some very large, others quite small, with period furniture, flounces, mouldings, medallions and state-of-the-art bathrooms (we liked the soft matt material of the fittings, the sober tiles with abstract motifs and the unusual coloured kimono bathrobes). The garden-facing rooms are our favourites. All corridors are pink, all bedroom doors green; behind them there is a great deal of blue, green and gold plush, ornate mirrors and extraordinary bedside lights with glass fringes. Last but first, the staff are exceptionally friendly and competent and do NOT indulge in Victorian delirium. (Sunday is a day of rest so fewer staff are on duty.)

Rooms: 39 with bathrooms.
Price: S 650-840F; D 700-940F;
TR 790-960F.
Breakfast: 40F.
Meals: None.
Metro: Ternes, Charles de Gaulle-Etoile (and RER).
Bus routes: 30 31 43 92 93
Car park: Hotel or Ternes.

The designer motto of Napoleon III's day was "Too much is not enough" (Trop n'est pas assez). Compare with our minimalist "Less is more" (Moins c'est plus).

Map No: 1

Hôtel Résidence Impériale   ★ ★ ★

155 avenue Malakoff
Paris
75116

Tel: (1)45 00 23 45
Fax: (1)45 01 88 82

Management: Pierre Salles.

In spite of the grand name this is far from being a snooty pretentious hostelry. Indeed, the young owner and his staff are enthusiastic, energetic and relaxed. He has renovated this old hotel from top to bottom, installed double glazing plus double windows and air conditioning — essential for rooms over the busy avenue — and chosen simple, made-to-measure furniture units in natural wood to make the best use of the space in each room. We particularly liked the original lamps, like leather-covered metal urns, giving off a softening light. The bedding is firm, the upholstery richly quilted, the curtains thick and generous. The rooms on the top floor have exposed roof timbers and sloping ceilings for a bit of character and those at the back look out over a row of small private gardens — so close yet so far from the hubbub of the International Conference Centre — and a rather lovely old curved redbrick building on a little side street. And when you go back down to street level, you can have the pleasure of your own small patio where Monsieur Salles soon hopes to see creepers creeping and blooms blooming again after renovation work. If you are cooped up all day in the Palais des Congrès or arrive by airport bus at the Porte Maillot, this is a nearby haven.

Rooms: 37 with bath or shower (inc disabled).
Price: S 656-746F; D/T 702-812F; TR 858-968F.
Breakfast: 55F with a large choice.
Meals: On request 100-300F.
Metro: Porte Maillot (+RER+Air France bus).
Bus routes: 73.
Car park: Palais des Congrès.

Malakoff was a bastion at Sebastopol that fell to Marshal MacMahon in the Crimean War after he (not Julius Caesar) had declared famously "J'y suis, j'y reste".

Map No: 1

St Augustin

•

Grévin waxworks museum

•

Department stores

•

Stock Exchange (Bourse)

Opera – Grands Boulevards

Hôtel de Beauharnais   ★ ★

51 rue de la Victoire
Paris
75009

Tel: (1)48 74 71 13
Fax: (1)44 53 98 80

Management: Madame Bey.

In a quiet side street (no need for double glazing here), Napoleon's beloved Joséphine de Beauharnais lived near this tiny ivy-covered hotel whose owner has such a vast personality. You will be entertained like a guest of the family and inducted in local lore of all sorts — make sure you have some time! The rooms, all different, reflect Madame Bey's passion for "brocante" and curiosities. She has a brilliant collection of old mirrors, each more baroque than the other and delights in framing pages from 19th-century magazines or calendars and turning them into features. One room is wholly decorated with a pink-framed print as inspiration. There is a series of opalescent pink-and-blue tinged Venetian light fittings to astound you. And two monumental beds, one with four white posts and a carved rack at the head sharing the space with a very feminine "Joséphine"-style dressing table; the other a great dark veneer-inlay set of pure 1920s carved pieces, including tall narrow curvy bevelled mirrors on either side of the majestic bed. Other rooms are less dramatic, some are quite small, but beds have good firm mattressess and high-quality floral sheets; showers are functional (behind sliding partitions only), storage space generally good. Above all, the atmosphere created by the Bey family is unforgettable.

Rooms: 17 with shower inc 13 with wc.
Price: S 300-340F; D 350 — 390F; TR 460-500F.
Breakfast: 25F.
Meals: None.
Metro: Chaussée d'Antin; RER + Roissybus Opéra-Auber.
Bus routes: 20 22 27 42 52 53 66 67
Car park: Galeries Lafayette.

Believe it or not, the Victoire is that of French king Philippe Auguste over England and her allies at Bouvines in 1214 — said to be the foundation of French nationhood.

(65)   **Map No:** 2

Hôtel Chopin ★★

10 boulevard Montmartre
(46 passage Jouffroy)
Paris
75009

Tel: (1)47 70 58 10
Fax: (1)42 47 00 70

Management: Monsieur Bidal.

The façade of the Chopin is a pure 1850s delight set across the end of a typical Parisian shopping arcade. The light airy lobby has always contained that green china pot beautifully copied in France when Chinoiserie was all the rage. Smiles are freely given, people are pleased to see you. Pianists beware — the piano hasn't been tuned for years. In your room, another unexpected pleasure greets you: all the rooms look out over courtyards (so no noise) and rooftops, the most stunning of which are the zinc expanses covering the Grévin waxworks museum (sleep quietly above bloody scenes of the French Revolution). I was dazzled by the roofer's craft here. The Salle des Papillons looks like a mediaeval multi-apsed chapel, the glass roof of the Passage Jouffroy like a vast upturned hull. The rooms are mostly a good size for a 2-star; the bathrooms have all been renovated, all in the same simple functional style. One of them has a "sulking" corner with chair. One corridor has three different colours, but not deliberately! Recently-renovated rooms have darker, modern colour schemes and ethnic materials; others, more pastel, are due to be redone. The furniture is plain and simple; there are some pretty white chairs with hand-applied transfer motifs and a clever cane table with two chairs "nesting" underneath it. The bedding is good firm foam. Monsieur Bidal's grandmother's water colours add class to this supremely pleasant, friendly hotel.

Rooms: 36 bath or shower (one with separate wc).
Price: S 405-435F; D 450-490F; TR 565F.
Breakfast: Buffet 36F.
Meals: None.
Metro: Richelieu-Drouot; RER Opéra-Auber.
Bus routes: 49 67 74 85
Car park: Drouot (special terms for hotel guests).

The moose's head over No 34 is made of papier maché: M Segas used to work in the theatre. He now sells a fascinating variety of antique canes...and a few genuine glass eyes.

Map No: 2

Hôtel Excelsior ***

16 rue Caroline
Paris
75017

Tel: (1)45 22 50 95
Fax: (1)45 22 59 88

Management: Monsieur Le Ralle.

Rather far from the city centre, on a quiet little street off the great boulevard memorably sung by Yves Montand, the excellent-value Excelsior has a façade that is worth a second look. It is listed, and rightly so with its wide openings, white mouldings and unselfconscious mosaic name, as a piece of 1920s Parisiana. Inside, there is a large garden with trees which for the moment is not open to guests as it is the after-school domain of the owners' sons. The rooms that give onto it obviously reap the benefits of leafiness, traffic silence and birdsong and Monsieur Le Ralle is examining ways of making it available for guests' use — it would be delightful of a summer's evening. He has chosen a late-medieval approach for the communal areas with beams, high-backed chairs and tapestries. Most rooms are a good size, sound-proofed and, on the lower floors, still have their moulded ceilings, fine fireplaces and ornate mirrors. The rooms onto the street with two windows each and small tables and chairs feel especially generous and have bold themes (green tartan carpeting and raspberry bedcovers; orange-red walls and curtains and lovely Chinese-pattern bedcovers). The carpet material that continues up over the bedhead is a clever unifying idea. The top-floor "attic" rooms with sloping ceilings and long roofscapes feel more cramped. Bathrooms vary according to the date of the last renovation. The programme continues. Again, the Excelsior is friendly good value.

Rooms: 22 with bath or shower.
Price: S 420F; D 450F.
Breakfast: 32F.
Meals: None.
Metro: Place de Clichy; RER Opéra-Auber.
Bus routes: 30 66
Car park: Europe.

In the 1860s Paris was growing fast. The village of Batignolles was gobbled up, the landowners were building madly — this one named his new street after his wife. Ah l'amour!

Map No: 1

Sacré Coeur

•

Place du Tertre & artists

•

Montmartre cemetery

•

Moulin Rouge

•

Funicular railway

Montmartre

 Visa

Hôtel le Bouquet de Montmartre **
1 rue Durantin
Paris
75018

Tel: (1)46 06 87 54
Fax: (1)46 06 09 09

Management: Madame Gibergues.

The Bouquet de Montmartre has been refurbished in keeping with its name (origin unknown), sweet and flowery and boudoir-like (the 3 façades should be done soon). A good 2-star hotel, it may not be to everyone's taste but it is all-of-a-piece, a lesson in a particular type of French interior. The black and white mosaic floor is eye-boggling; the decor is all flock "brocade" wallpaper, glue-on mouldings and curlicues, curvy sideboards and Louis XVI chairs. The breakfast room is lit by large windows onto the square...and vast numbers of mottled-glass light fittings on walls and ceiling. This careful decoration covers the stairs and landings, with lights set in niches and moulded ceiling wells. The original 1920s banisters are painted white and gold to match and all doors are "leather"-padded. The rooms vary — some are still being renovated — but the design principle is beds in alcoves with myriad little cupboards around, plus hanging space, and candle-shaped lights. Curtains and bedcovers are generally the same material — red and green striped satiny stuff or muted blue and beige velvet or textured ethnic print — and the newer bath/shower-rooms treated in two-coloured mosaic tiling. Mattresses are firm foam and recent. The Gibergues family work hard at keeping up with their large house and still have time to sit and chat with their guests. Friendly, simple, in one of the prettiest squares in Paris and excellent value.

Rooms: 36 with bath or shower.
Price: S/D 340-410F; TR 440F.
Breakfast: 30F.
Meals: None.
Metro: Abbesses, Pigalle; RER Gare du Nord.
Bus routes: 30 54 67 68 74 95
Car park: Place Clichy.

You emerge from the metro at Abbesses under one of the finest remaining Art Nouveau canopies by Hector Guimard deliciously blending into its leafy surroundings.

Map No: 2

Hôtel Caulaincourt *

2 square Caulaincourt
63/65 rue Caulaincourt, Paris
75018

Tel: (1)46 06 42 99
Fax: (1)46 06 48 67

Management: Monsieur Hacène.

    Visa

When the bottom of Paris is sweltering and unbreathable, come up to the top, to Montmartre, and perch on the airy hillside. The Caulaincourt gives onto two steep slopes — one of those vertiginous staircases on one side and a scruffy, wild woody slope of a communal garden at the back. It is a superbly basic place to stay — at these prices, what else would you expect? — in an exquisitely privileged position. The "mountain air" sweeps through the warren-like corridors and the rooms are simple and spotless. The garden is virtually unusable but a blessed source of fresh air and quiet (except when the teenagers in the next-door building blast a momentary techno-rave over their mammoth decibel machines, but this is short-lived). Indeed, there is no double glazing and no need for it. This is the peaceful and very bourgeois part of Montmartre yet you can walk up to the Place du Tertre and the Sacré Coeur in 5 minutes. The lobby and breakfast room, directly off the little leafy impasse (with its excellent café-restaurant), are as straightforward, almost bare, as the rest. Rooms are sparsely furnished with decent firm bedding, candlewick bedcovers, very adequate bedside lights and shower-rooms (where applicable — more are being installed every year) and totally harmless wallpapers. No frills but excellent value and a clear desire to provide good basic service.

Rooms: 50 with basin, shower or shower & wc.
Price: S basin 129F; D basin 159F; D shower 199F; D shower wc 249F.
Breakfast: 30F.
Meals: None.
Metro: Lamarck-Caulaincourt; RER Gare du Nord.
Bus routes: 80
Car park: Rue Damrémont.

Having renounced his peerage, Caulaincourt was a foot soldier during the Revolution, an ardent follower of Napoleon, a friend of Tsar Alexander, and still managed to die in his bed.

Map No: 2

 Visa

Hôtel Prima Lepic   * *
29 rue Lepic
Paris
75018

Tel: (1)46 06 44 64
Fax: (1)46 06 66 11

Management: Madame Renouf.

A red warren where all the rooms are as different from each other as the people of Montmartre. The Moulin de la Galette and its cabaret dancers are close by; wealthy modern "artists" (show biz) live up on the smart avenue; the hotel's wonderful fresco portrays a typical tramp with his bottle of "gros rouge" to hand on the bench. The house follows the hill, like everything else except the Sacré Coeur, and some balustrades, floors and doors are at wild angles. Madame Renouf loves the place and her job — this is careful hands-on management — and has refurbished it with pieces found on country markets or made to measure for her rooms. She favours bright wall papers, coordinated curtain and canopy materials (several beds have overhead drapes and big bows), white bedcovers, rustic wooden or white-painted rattan cupboards and chairs. There are some more traditional rooms; brass lamps, old carved bedside tables and gilt-framed mirrors abound. The largest rooms are those ending in 5. They have grand double doors, two windows, perhaps a balcony or a marble fireplace. Others are smaller and bath or shower-rooms are neatly functional, some with folding doors only; the old walls are pretty thin. The ground floor has a fine mural of the high points of the village and a conservatory atmosphere with deep lightwells illuminating myriad indoor plants (real and artificial), white garden furniture and a cage with 3 parrots, all perching on the outside... and all fake. Sympathique quoi!

Rooms: 35 + 3 suites with bath or shower.
Price: S 350-370F; D 380-420F; TR 450-500F; ST (for 4-5) 700F.
Breakfast: 40F.
Meals: None.
Metro: Abbesses, Pigalle; RER Gare du Nord.
Bus routes: 30 54 67 68 74 95
Car park: Place Marie Blanche.

Rue Lepic bustles with the little shops that are dying out elsewhere — Montmartre is truly a village still, albeit within a vast "developed" city.

Map No: 2

INDEX

ORDER FORM

(The more you buy the less they cost!)

Name _____

Address _____

_____

Postcode _____

"Alastair Sawday's Guide to Special Paris Hotels"

1 copy	(£8.95)	_____
2 copies @ £7.50 each	(£15.00)	_____
3 copies @ £7.00 each	(£21.00)	_____
4 or more copies @ £6.50 each	(£ .)	_____

"Alastair Sawday's Guide to French Bed & Breakfast"
(see announcement after map section at beginning of book)

1 copy	(£11.95)	_____
2 copies @ £10.50 each	(£21.00)	_____
3 copies @ £9.50 each	(£28.50)	_____
4 or more copies @ £9.00 each	(£ .)	_____

(Postage & Packing FREE)

TOTAL   _____

Signed _____ Date _____

I enclose cheque payable to :
Alastair Sawday Publishing, 44 Ambra Vale East, Bristol BS8 4RE, UK.